First edition, November 2, 2017

Psychology of how to invest

The best lesson for private investors

Vincent van Roon
© 2017 Vincent van Roon

All rights reserved. Nothing in this publication may be reproduced, stored in an automated database, or made public, in any form or by any means, electronic, mechanical, photocopying, recording, or any other means without the prior written permission of the author.

All rights reserved. No part of this publication may be reproduced, stored in a retrieval system, or transmitted, in any form or by any means, electronic, mechanical, photocopying, recording or otherwise, without the prior written permission of the author.

Index

1. About the author
2. Preface
3. Everyone can be an investor
4. What not to do
5. What to do
6. Returning trade effects
7. My investments
8. Epilogue

1. About the author

Vincent van Roon (1982) started investing with his twelfth. Through his uncle Jan he got the basic principles explained and soon investing became a major part of his life. Since then he has been following the financial markets. Vincent likes long term investing, because that ultimately ranks the most. In order to keep the tension in mind, he invests more adventurous with 20% of his portfolio. In the early years, Vincent invested primarily in investment funds. Then he switched to individual stocks, options, turbo`s and futures. It soon turned out that investing was not so easy at all. Although Vincent had gained a lot of knowledge about financial markets due to his great interest, he did not succeed in making a profit. He found out that the factor 'psychology' had a negative impact on his investment profit. Vincent is then going to investigate what the emotional influence of investors is on investment results. When it turned out that investor's emotional behavior mainly determines the investment result, Vincent has completely reversed his investment strategy. After years of loss, this has resulted in profitable investment.
Through this book, Vincent wants to give investors knowledge about how to invest better and what not to do.
Vincent writes this book for beginner investors and investors, who have been active on the stock market for a long time. He has written this book completely independent and describes, in its own way, the effects of investor motions on investment results. There are many books written about the technical theory of investing, but not about the emotional side of investing. That's why Vincent decided to write this book based on his own experiences.

2. Preface

Approximately 80% of private investors, acting independently on the stock exchange, incur losses. However, after my investigation, not the knowledge about investing, but the investor's motivation, causes the majority of private investors to suffer losses.
The pressure that individuals impose themselves on investing well is huge. Losses are extremely disappointing, and in today's society people find money the most important. Therefore, 'will' and 'can' an investor not lose. This emotion ensures that investors make decisions that a professional investor will never take. Finally, a professional investor does not have the emotional pressure of a private investor. A professional does not invest with his private ability, but with the ability of another and is also neat at the end of the workday, and carefree going home. Professional investors also take profit from the mistakes that private investors make on the stock market. The professionals focus on the foundations and not on the emotion.

There are many books in which private investors can acquire knowledge about investing. But with only knowledge you are not ready to invest. Even more important is to keep your investor emotions under control. For years, I have not had my investor emotions under control and belonged to the 80% of investors who suffered loss. Fortunately, I could change my mind. I learned from my mistakes and, after my research, used a different investment strategy.
I am convinced that, with the information from my book, many investors will get better results. I have written this book for both the beginning investor and investors who have been active for the stock market for longer, but who can not keep their emotions under control.

The book is made up of two parts. The first part tells you what you better not do as an investor and the second part deals with how you better should invest. After that, I have described a number of recurring stock market effects, which you can use as an investor. Finally, I give you a look at my own investments. In the book I described both my own experiences and other practical situations.

3. Everyone can be an investor

Many people ask before investing if it is difficult. Often people think that investing is for the fast boys in tailoring. With backward hair and a pulsating appearance, they will know exactly what share you have to buy. However, that is not true. The type of person I describe is the perfect seller. In other words, the investment adviser.
Everyone has the same chance at the stock market. Self-investing is provided for everyone. It does not matter what education you have enjoyed, whether you are old or young, woman or man. Everybody can invest. Of course, some people have a more sense of investing than the other. But even that is a given, which can be changed. Finally, you can learn the basics and increase your knowledge, if you want. And then there is still no one who can predict the stock prices. Whatever you know about investing, it does not determine that you can say with certainty what will happen tomorrow at the stock market. Someone who is sure that shares will increases or decreases, therefore, you should not take seriously. This investor can at most have a well-founded suspicion why a share will rise or fall. I have also said a number of times before, knowing that a certain share would rise or fall. Often that went well, but not always. And the more you feel good, the more you wise yourself, you can predict your prices. And with that overpower you can go into the fog later. You can overestimate yourself, which ultimately leads to irresponsible investing and possibly also results in heavy money losses.
For people who do not yet have experience with investing, it is wise to first learn a lot about investing on the internet. What is a share? What's happening on the stock market? In addition, if you follow a slanted eye on stock quotes live, you start to understand what is actually happening on the stock market and what investing mean.

"Investing is as difficult as you make it yourself"

A next step is to join an investment competition. The so-called *dry investment* ensures that you see what happens to your money when you make a profit and loss. That way, it will soon become clear that you probably notice that it is not so easy to make a profit on the stock market. And it's better to experience this with fake money than directly with your worthy cents. Then you can decide whether self-investing is something for you or that you immediately decide to throw the towel in the ring.

Various investment competitions have been organized in recent years. Usually this competition takes a couple of weeks. You can invest in stocks, options and etf's. I have also participated in these stock markets a number of times. I used to do that as an investor in my early years. At the moment, I am only investing with real money. I still know that for the first time, I participated in the Eurobench.com stock market competition around 1999. That was a different kind of competition than what I just described. In December, prior to the competition year, you chose the top five shares, which you expected the best to perform the coming year. It is therefore pure speculation and a dose of luck you certainly need. The first year I won the competition and the second year I became second. I won a nice amount of money, then, ƒ 400, – . After that, I participated in a stock market competition a few more times, but after the first two stock markets competitions of Eurobench.com, my luck was gone.

"Investment advisors have the knowledge and keep their emotions under control"

Do investment advisers really perform better than private investors? That is not possible to say with only YES or NO. Investment advisors know very much about investing. In fact, they are almost all a lot further than any private investor as well. They know all the small details and investment opportunities without any problems. However, they also can not predict stock prices. And that's what matters. In order to invest successfully, a private investor does not need as much knowledge as an investment adviser. The basic principles are often enough. What added value does an investment advisor have? Mostly mentally, investment advisors are better than the average private investor. Individuals often act on the stock exchange, unconsciously, emotionally on events, while investment advisors focus on the facts. Someone who has enough money and can not control his investor emotions can therefore give his money better to a professional adviser.

As mentioned earlier, investment advisors can not predict stock prices. There are different calculation methods, which sometimes predict another stock price. I now know enough investment advisors, who perform worse than individuals. However, you must have steel nerves when investing independently. Losses hurt and nobody corrects you when you making unthinkable investment decisions. In contrast to investing by yourself, the investment adviser is responsible for managing you. The investment advisor thus has an important function. I call an investment advisor often a *risk adviser*, because he just makes the difference about that compare to private investors. When you want to invest yourself, it's very important to keep yourself in control.

"Do you have your emotions under control as an investor? "

When I occasionally speak to other investors, I often get the question: What should I buy, what is the perfect share? However, there is no clear answer. To answer this question, ask yourself a few questions first:

- What do I want?
- How much risk do I want to take?
- How much time do I have?
- What is my investment goal?

These four questions are essential to determining the best investment. Finally, every investment has its own risk profile and its potential for return. For example, do you want to receive a dividend, or do you just want a company to invest the dividend to speed up business growth? This is not black-on-white on paper, but this teaches you by gaining experience when you are active longer on the stock market.

In addition, you must ask yourself whether investing is simply a hobby or it's about making money. This determines how much time you invest in investing. Someone who invests purely to make returns can often invest better in the long run. While an investor, who likes to follow the market and makes it a hobby, can also actively invest for some.

Once you have answered the above questions, it's time to make an investment plan. An investment advisor makes the same plan, but if you invest independently, you have to do this yourself. It is essential for your ultimate success. It is very important to know in advance what you invest and what choices you want to make. You run the risk of becoming a big chaos, resulting in loss. Without a plan, you are likely to choose different risks and types of investments each time you would probably never have taken with an investment plan. In short, you must have a goal. Perhaps your goal is making money for retirement or you may want to work fewer hours in your job. You can still know so much about investment, but without a clear investment plan you will always lose.

Once you have acquired enough investment knowledge and have made an investment plan so that you can keep your investment motives down, you're ready to enter the stock market. Do not let yourself go through the craziness of the day, but stick to your plan. An investment plan is not by definition profitable, as this is mainly due to the quality of the plan. In this book, I give handles for making a successful investment plan.

I describe these principles on the basis of my investment experience of the last 21 years and especially where I went well and wrong. I want to save you for the mistakes I made. In addition, I'll show you the chances, which will make you profitable. If, after reading this book, you still have to make the mistakes that I describe in the book, it's time to tell yourself to stop. Perhaps it is better to place your money with an investment adviser. However, I am convinced that after reading this book, anyone can be successful at the stock market. Everyone can invest, provided you have gained enough knowledge and can keep your investor emotions under control. For the first part, about the information about the stock market, I will refer you to websites or other books. The second part, the emotions of investors, I hope to add you through this book everything you need.

4. What not to do

Since the nineties, more and more private investors, who take their investment decisions independently, are active on the stock market. However, the number of private investors decreases in the years when the stock market is poor, but on the other hand, it increases again if the stock market is good. This shows that private investors are fully influenced by the sentiment. Investors often act as opposed to how you should act as an investor. And that's going wrong. This chapter discusses the negative impact of investor motions on investors' decisions. After all, you can know a lot about investing, but if you do not control your investor emotions, you do not have anything about your gained knowledge. The mistakes that I discuss below you can better not make if you want to invest successfully on the stock market.

Too much trading

A major mistake made by private investors is too much trading on the stock market. Driven by emotion, investors take more risk by acting more. There are several emotions why investors decide to sell one investment and buy another for a buyback. Looking at stock prices causes the brain to be more vulnerable to investor motions. It turns out that the more volatile share is, the more often investors are trading. From a psychological point of view, that is quite logical. The more volatile one share, the more chances are to enter or exit at a favorable price. A share, which is less volatile, will provide for less psychological pressure to sell. Rest on the stock market also takes care of rest in the head. Below is an example of practice.

The Altice share is currently one of the most volatile shares in the Dutch headindex AEX. The purchase price of the share is for an investor for example € 25, -. The share rises to € 30, -. Then, however, the share drops to € 24, -. The investor got a psychological attack because he could sell with a profit of € 5. By contrast, he currently has a paper loss of € 1, -. This course of trade has a consequence for the decision that he makes at the next price movement. The share will quickly recover to € 28, -. The investor decides to sell the stock, because he is very happy that he can sell with profit. He has previously seen that a huge win of € 5, - disappeared as snow for the sun and he even suffered loss. Due to the rapid recovery, the investor could still sell a nice profit.

From this example it turns out that many investors are emotionally influenced between having a profit or loss. If an investor first has a paper profit, which turns into loss, the investor strikes his head. Why did not I make a profit? That's what the investor is asking for. Many investors then assume the next possibility that the share is again in the plus to sell the share. Having a profit is finally a much better feeling than having a loss. Regardless of the level of profit or loss.

Actually, this kind of psychological warfare is the biggest problem with you. The share of Altice could also continue to rise to € 30, - or € 35, -. The probability that the share would fall from the selling price of € 28, - is just as big as that the share would increase. Only in the head of the investor, this is not the case. The investor has now sold and purchases another, or sometimes the same share, one day later. The same ritual then repeats itself.

With shares that are much less volatile, the rapid purchasing and sales effect is less. A share like KasBank (Dutch company) is not volatile. If the share does not move fast, the investor's brain to act quickly will not be stimulated. Finally, there is no sense of losing profit by not gaining time on time. Long-term price movements have a less significant effect on the investor's brain. Daily or weekly fluctuations in prices have a lot more impact than fluctuations, which take months or years. In spite of the fact that the level of losses, or lost profits, in the long run is often greater than in the short term. Take good care of volatile shares. The fast price movements cause you to unconsciously sell and sell much faster than you would like to do in advance. And the faster you lose the loss, or the lost profit, by buying a new share directly, the less controlled that decision is. Because you want to quickly make your new purchase, you have paid less attention to find out if the share is actually buyable. The investor's brain is purely focused on the pursuit of profit.

In addition to taking more risk, taking quicker and uncontrolled investment decisions costs and sells a lot of money. There are two factors that make you lose money on every purchase and sale. You start, as it were, every transaction with loss.

First, you pay commission on the buy and sale of the share. In relative terms, the cost of shares is less high than for options or futures. Despite the fact that the costs for trades are getting lower, commission costs are still higher than you would think. I have experienced this myself.

Beginning this century, when I traded a lot in shares and options, I did a transaction almost daily. At that time I had an investment portfolio of approximately € 10,000, -. Despite the fact that I often had a track record, my final return proved to be quite a challenge. At the end of the year I was curious about how that came and I calculated my commission fees for that year. At the time, I had paid to my broker the scary amount of € 1,800. It was therefore not a surprise for me that my gains eventually resulted in a net loss. From that year I started to trade less. And I have not regret that until now.

A second cost item is the spread of purchase and sale. The spread is the difference in the buying and selling price of the share, option, or any other derivative investment product.

ING

Volume	bid in	late	volume
2.525	14.53	14.55	500
5.900	14.52	14.56	2.500
1.500	14.51	14.58	5.590
2.660	14.49	14.60	1.150
8.905	14.48	14.61	2.890

The above example shows that you can buy ING for € 14.55 and can sell for € 14.53. Since you buy one time in one investment and ever sell once, this means a start loss of € 0.02. At first, that does not seem to be much, but for investors who do a lot of trading, this makes a big difference at the end of the year.

ING is a liquid share. In the case of illiquid shares, which are often listed on the local market, the spread is much greater, which means that the start loss is also greater. Many trades in illiquid shares thus results in a greater chance of loss in the final result.

In addition to shares, a spread also applies to derivative investment products, such as options and futures. In relative terms, the spread on derivative products is much larger than on shares. Although derivative products are much more volatile than stocks, making it easier for you to start off, investors need to realize that the chance of ultimate profit is much smaller than loss.

Often, after your new transaction, you could better keep your old investment. Trading costs a lot of money and your new investment does not necessarily have to be better than your old investment.

Taking too must risks

Investing is taking risks. In addition, each investment has its own risk level of risk. Investing is accepting the risk of losing money, but it means that you can achieve an above average profit compared to have money on savings. Return and risk go hand in hand. The more risk you take, the greater the chance of more return. If you do not accept the opportunity to lose money, you can better not start investing. Free money does not exist at once. There must be something about it and that is the risk of a financial disappointment. Sometimes, however, the risks you take may be too big. Sometimes that is aware of a too big risk, but it often goes unconsciously. Usually, you only know afterwards that the risk you took has been too big. And that can occur on all types of investments, such as stocks and options. The moment your investment is on a profit, your risk often diminishes. When your position turns out to be a big loss, it's just starting to realize that you might have taken too much risk. There are a number of features that show that the investment you took is irresponsible.

First, investors with an irresponsible investment look more often at stock prices than when there is no irresponsible investment. Investors can always refresh the screen every hour or, in some cases, to see every minute how the prices are. Certainly in the case of options and similar kind of products, whose fluctuations are many times larger than shares, some investors leave the computer screen at no time. Nowadays, you have apps on your phone, so you can watch the prices anywhere. On the one hand, a glorious invention, on the other hand, has resulted in much more buys and sales by individuals. Unlimited nervous to peer to your computer screen or phone does not benefit your investment choices.

"The night's pains about your investment mean you have a completely irresponsible position"

If we go further, investors will find the sleepless nights. This step goes a long way further than the frequent tracking of prices. At the moment that an investor can not sleep because he constantly thinks of his investment, something goes wrong. The investment in question is completely irresponsible. *Irresponsible* in the sense of the risk of the investment, but also in the level of investment. The latter is actually the cause of an irresponsible investment. With a good spread, investment with an above average risk is not at all bad.

However, if your risky investment exceeds a quarter or more of your portfolio, you can say that it is irresponsible.

In the past, I have more often taken irresponsible risks by speculating on options. I have a lot of examples here. Sometimes I made big profits, but in other cases, my irresponsible investment resulted in a huge loss. My biggest, irresponsible investment I took when I was 21 years old. At that time, I lived at home with my parents, worked full time for a bank and had built up a large amount of money. At least, compared to my peers. At that time, I traded in stock options. At the time, the risk of just shares was too boring for me and I was looking for even higher returns. Due to the fact that I had low fixed costs, I could take irreparable high risks. In the beginning, when I started trading with options, I did this for a few hundred euros. Soon, this went on to a few thousand euros. Success increases confidence in yourself and thereby losing the fear of losing money too. When you're successful, you're taking more risk. One day I was so sure that the AEX would increase, that I decided to buy call options on the AEX for € 10,000. I had never invested with such a large amount of money. But I was so sure that I took all the risks that an investor could take. However, *be sure* does not exist, that's something I only later found out. The motility of that particular option series was very large because it involved day options. My position would still expire that same day. I had invested the full amount, which was on my securities account, in daily options on the AEX. Not knowing what to expect.

"I bought for $ 10,500, - 50 call options on the AEX, which would expire the same day ..."

I took the position when I was at my job behind my desk. I worked in a bank's call center, so I was constantly busy with calling by customers. In between, I looked at the AEX index every two minutes. A colleague, an older man, also realized that I was constantly switching between my screen and the AEX rate screen. I had to watch out that colleagues did not notice this because, in that department, the atmosphere was not going very well. And of course, it's not the intention to actively trading while you're working. Not half an hour later I decided to walk outside for fear of committing my broker to sell my position. At that time, there was no mobile internet yet. In total, I earned € 1,100, - which, in relative terms, is not much based on the risk I had taken. This half hour was probably the most nervous half hour I've ever experienced. Despite the nice profits, I wanted that I did not take the risk. However, I have learned to never take such an irresponsible position anymore. I've been able to laugh afterwards and have a nice story to tell the pub.

Let losses run bigger, and cut profits

That, as an investor, you make both profit and loss on a share is nothing more than normal. Even guru Warren Buffet is not a word-seeker and often loses money, even though people sometimes think differently. However, it is important to make more profit than loss. And of course, profits need to be greater than losses. It sounds logical, but in real life it often turns out to be the opposite. The investor's brain is responsible for this. It is therefore important mentally not to make the same mistakes as other investors. Investors, who share profit, are quickly inclined to win the profits. You do not want to lose that profit anymore. Imagine that the share drops, so you've just lost the profit you had before. And that is very painful to the investor's brain. The fear of losing the achieved price gain causes many investors to sell the share too fast. However, it often happens that the first increase is only a sign that the share can go up much further. The trend upwards has just been used and the share is still increasing further in weeks and months afterwards.
On the other hand, many investors take a lot of different decisions when a price loss is taking place. When investors are at a loss, they are just waiting for the share to rise again. Investors do not want to sell at a loss. The uncontrolled risk causes the share to fall even further before the investor only intervenes. Suppose the share is now

40% loss, another mechanism starts in the investor's brain. The fear of the big loss increases and therefore the investor sells. The investor is angry. And often it happens when the share is at the lowest point. Because the investor can no longer bear the loss from a psychological point of view, he is selling financially and mentally. While, from a fundamental point of view, the share is often undervalued and therefore worthwhile.

Investors often act as opposed to how you should actually act in the stock market. Pure from the psychological pressure he makes these wrong decisions. Looking from a basic perspective, he should have done the opposite.

Higher stakes

A major mistake made by private investors is to take on even bigger positions. For stocks, options and other financial instruments, this is not recommended. If investors have made a profit, they often take the normal bet plus invest the profit in another share. Due to the increased intake, the chances of big winnings will rise, but also the chances of big losses. Investors are now convinced by realized profits and think it's even better to invest more the next time. On the other hand, that also applies. When investors lose money, they want as quickly as possible recover the lost money. As a result, they take place at greater risk by investing more money. That way they think recoup faster the loss. Also, the risk of even greater loss will increase substantially. Investors are attracted by their emotions and take ever greater risks by investing more and to invest in more risky assets. However, this strategy is wrong. Of course it is possible to create a lot of profit, but in practice, it turns out much more often wrong than right.

Compare it into a casino. If you play roulette in a casino, you can gamble for example on black and red. Suppose you start with € 100,-. Below you see an example of how lot of players in the casino gambling throughout the evening.

€ 100, -, bet € 10, - on red: you win! ... you have got € 110, -
€ 110, -, bet € 10, - on black: you win! ... you have got € 120, -
€ 120, -, bet € 10, - on red: you win ... you have got € 130, -

It goes very well with this gambler tonight. Three out of three bets he gambled right. He decides € 30, - to put in, because he is doing so well tonight. And if he's right, the profit is increasing so rapidly that has € 160, - !

€ 130, -, bet € 30, - on red: fault ... you have got € 100, -.
€ 100, -, bet € 10, - on black: fault ... you have got only € 90, - left.

It went so well in the casino, but suddenly the player is at a loss. In his emotion he bet more because he wants to make up the loss as quickly as possible and get back to profit. If he places a € 40, - bet and win, he is back at his old high level of € 130, -.

€ 90, -, bet € 40, - on red: fault ... you have only € 50, - left.

The odds were nice, but the gambler forgets in his emotion that he, by this loss, even is in a worse state then before. He decides to bet everything. It is so often gone wrong, it must go well again? And with that small investment of € 10, - it finally takes ages before he gains resists. If he wins a large deposit, he is at least breaking even again.

€ 50, -, bet € 50, - on red: fault ... and you've lost everything.

This situation, as here in the casino, happens more often than you can imagine. And on the stock exchange this works equally. Many private investors do not invest for the long term, but speculate on price movements. If you bet with options and futures on the stock market, then is the chance that the above situation will happen very big. Investing in short term options and futures is very similar to roulette in the casino. Probably many will disagree with this, but the facts are, to me, just that way. Because with shares, aside from bankruptcy, you can not lose the entire investment, compared to the roulette at the casino.

"Never go to increase your investment in the stock market after profit or loss"

It is therefore advisable, both in profit and loss, not to increase your investment. Obviously, this can lead to profits, but in practice, it is more often wrong than right. Not for nothing does 80% of the individuals loose on the stock market. If the gambler example, had never raised his stake in the casino, but constant € 10, - had inlaid, he had € 90, - left. That was just a loss of € 10, - instead of losing everything.

Resources

For private investors losing money is very heavy. Losing your own money is not nice. It is in the human being that losing money is as a tremendous sense of failure. Maybe that's a good thing, because otherwise we would never have made economic progress. Investors are all too happy to cover their losses. Selling a losing position investors find often heavy. You are namely confronted directly with your loss. But take loss, is often the best cure. Often investors do the opposite of what they should do: they just buy extra shares. So instead of selling the stock because the company is for example in bad shape, they just buy shares. This, with only one goal: bringing the average price down, so the chance of coming quickly gain is greater. This is called 'price middling'.

"Instead of selling a losing position, investors often buy extra shares"

Investors often apply this technique to stocks that go down like falling knives. With the feeling that the share now really reached the bottom brings investors to buy the shares. Investors sometimes try three, four or five times to middle the price. Often, this results in large losses. Greater losses than investors normally might wear. In his emotion he was purely trying to get his right. But you have to think rationally. Just do not be concerned with profit or loss. Thinking of the share going to do the next time. Does it make sense to hold it? If an investor does not own the stock at first, he would never buy the share, whose price thunders together. Only because of the fact that the investor already owns the stock, he decides to buy the share. The investor will take too much risk, and in his subconscious he goes 'all-in'. In some situations it goes well, but in too many cases it is completely in the fog.

A good example is the share Fagron. After the third quarter results of 2015 the share dropped from € 42, - to € 35, -. Internet forums showed that many investors found it a good time to buy a few shares. Subsequently, the proportion dropped the weeks continues. On many forums investors told that they wanted to 'price middle', because the share was very far sunk. The share listed now € 25, -. And that was a lot lower than the average purchase price. By means of € 25, - decreased average purchase price, which, at a recovery rate, faster gains could be made. However, these investors underestimated the trouble Fagron left entirely to themselves pass. The company insisted namely not so well. The resulting decline in the share price was quite logical. However, investors had only the numbers which they had bought in their head and how many losses they had made.

"The focus on the loss makes investors blindly"

The share Fagron stands at the time of writing at € 8, -. Often it happens that investors decide to sell at a sharply lower rate everything. This is due to the psychological pressure, which is discussed in the previous chapter. The investor, who has followed the scenario above, has done everything wrong, he could do wrong.

Buy 100 shares Fagron at € 40, -
Additional buy (price middle) 100 shares Fagron at € 35, - (average drops to € 37.50)
Additional buy (price middle) 100 shares Fagron at € 25, - (average drops to € 33.33)

Current price Fagron € 8, -.

100 shares Fagron: loss € 3.200, -
300 shares Fagron: loss € 7.600, -

If you did not buy extra shares the loss was "only" € 3.200, -. Investors, who have bought extra shares to middle the price lower, are having a loss of up to € 7600, -.

It is apparent from the above example, in that means is rather dangerous. The odds for a recovery of the share is larger, but the loss to a further weakening for an average investor insurmountable great. The above average risk, which you choose, makes yourself, as an investor, a ticking time bomb. Ones it will go completely   y wrong. Investors choose precisely the funds in stocks, hard bags, but those are the companies where something is not going well. Means you had better avoid the vast majority of cases.

Leverage products

Who wants faster and bigger profits than is possible only with stocks? It will be a surprise if not everyone raises his hand. Investing is ultimately to achieve the highest possible efficiency. Leveraged products can be made much more efficient than equity. The best known and most popular product in The Netherlands is the 'turbo'. It took some time before the popularity of this product took off, but the turbo is very popular right now. Many private investors invest in turbos, because, as I started, there are significant gains to be made. However, surveys show that by far most people make loss by using turbo`s. And that is not surprising, because each investor already at the inception of the position starts losing.
With the purchase of a turbo, you pay only a small part of the share. The increase or decrease of the share is the same as when you buy the share.

Example:
ING share costs € 13, -

- Turbo 12 (€ 12 - the stop loss level, and € 11,50 the level of funding).

You decide to buy on the turbo at a price of
€ 1.50 (€ 13 - - € 11.50)

Situation:

1. ING shares rose to € 14,20. The price of the turbo became € 2.70.   (€ 14,20 - € 11,50). If you decide to sell you get a profit of 80 % (purchase price € 1.50 and the sale price € 2.70)
2. ING shares fell to € 11.80. It thus does not run well with your turbo. The stop-loss level of € 12 , - is achieved. This is your turbo sold automatically and terminated at € 12 , - at the rate of € 0.50 (€ 12 , - - € 11,50). Your loss is therefore 67 % (€ 1.50 - € 0.50).

An investor makes when opening his turbo position a direct loss. This is because he pays brokerage fees, he had to buy at the bid price and in addition interest will be calculated from the level of funding.

- Commission costs : these are usually the same cost as for share transactions .
- Spread : in the above case, the spread of the turbo was € 1.48 to € 1.52.
- Daily corrects the level of funding, because it is calculated on the amount of interest. Thereby increasing the funding level and the value of your turbo automatically worth less.

Due to the fact that, when opening and maintaining a turbo position, are very much adverse financial consequences, it is not surprising that most of the investors suffered losses with turbos. Turbos so often sound better than reality shows. If you still decide to be investing in turbos, do it with a small amount and with a stoploss (of appropriate turbo), which is far removed from the current rate. Relatively speaking it cheaper and safer for investors.

An emerging product category leveraged trading is the binary option. Providers of binary options allow the product to prevent a serious investment, but that is not true. Binary options are on indices, equities, currencies and commodities. With these options, you speculate on the rise or fall of the underlying asset, the AEX. And you do for a period of, for example one hour, four hours or a day. The term of binary options is usually quite short. There are two outcomes: you're right or you're wrong. If you're right, you win the predetermined percentage, usually around 80%. If you lose, you lose the entire bet. You can compare this with the roulette table in the casino.

"You have more chance of winning at the casino than investing in binary options"

However, at the roulette table in the casino profits are higher if you win. With binary options, you win about 80% if you're right, but you lose 100% if you're wrong. In the casino you lose 100% if you're wrong, but you win 97.3% if you do it right. In roulette, the number gives *zero* ensure that your chances by betting on black or red, 36 on 37.

You obviously think you can predict the price of, for example, the AEX well. Especially if you win, you start believing in yourself. However, you should win more often than lose to make a profit, as shown by the example below, where you win five times as well lose five times.

Deposit € 10, -: profit represents 80% profit = € 18, - return
Deposit € 10, -: loss means full inlay lost
Deposit € 10, -: loss means full inlay lost
Deposit € 10, -: loss means full inlay lost
Deposit € 10, -: profit represents 80% profit = € 18, - return
Deposit € 10, -: profit represents 80% profit = € 18, - return
Deposit € 10, -: loss means full inlay lost
Deposit € 10, -: loss means full inlay lost

Deposit € 10, -: profit represents 80% profit = € 18, - return
Deposit € 10, -: profit represents 80% profit = € 18, - return

Deposit € 100, - and you will receive € 90, - return. So you lose a whole € 10, - if you win as often as losing.

This example show that you have to watch out us binary options. Leverage products are mainly intended to win the bank or broker and lose the investor.

Buying short term options

In my early years as investor I mostly invested in options, my favorite. Focused on the huge profits that could be achieved, I bought mostly short out of the money call options. And that is precisely the type of option, which has probability the biggest chance of loss. This is a mistake that most investors take.
Investors are guided naturally by the huge profit opportunities that arise. Investors also focused far too little on the risk associated with the relevant investment. The dollar signs and greed push the risk effect to the background. Full of optimism, investors assumed that the gain, for they are indeed too smart to suffer losses, they think. Many investors buy just out of the money options with short maturities. See the example below.

The share price of Royal Dutch Shell is € 23.60 in November 2015 and you expect the stock to rise. You have to choose out of some option series and you decide to choose for out of the money options, which will expire next month.

Call December € 23.00, price € 0.94 (in the money option)
Call December € 23.50, price € 0.63 (at the money option)
Call December € 24.00, price € 0.40 (out of the money option)

The disadvantage of a short-term out of the money option is that the share price must rise a lot in a short time. This is of course possible, but the probability that it would not happen, is much greater.

> "Because it is unlikely that the share is rising rapidly and much, investors often make a loss with out of the money options"

A small four weeks later the option series expires though. Below you will see examples of the possible expiration price of Royal Dutch Shell.

Situation:

- RDS price € 23 , - : the price is less than € 24, - series, making your option expires worthless, you lost everything.
- RDS price € 24 - : the price is equal to € 24, - series, so now your option expires worthless, you lost everything.
- RDS price € 25 -: The price is € 1, - higher than you € 24, - series, will get you € 1, - return, pull off your deposit of € 0.40 , then like you'd have a gross profit from € 0.60.

The exercise price is € 24, -.
The premium you pay is € 0.40.
The cost you pay to your broker, is approximately € 0.10.
Together is € 24.50. The current price is € 23.60.

The share of Royal Dutch Shell must rise at least 3.8% to come from your initial loss. From that share price on, you make profit. So even though the share price rises, it does not mean you automatically call

option to gain state. In a short time, out of the money call option has to increase so very sharply, before making your profits.
Therefore, it is much wiser to choose a call option which is in or at the money. Despite that your final profit is likely to be smaller by the lower leverage, the risk is also much smaller. The share namely needs to rise much less fast. The much wiser to choose a call option with a longer maturity. Although it costs slightly more money, the odds of winning are ultimately much higher.

Overestimate yourself

It is very dangerous when investors say to be sure that a particular price movement is coming. These investors overestimate themselves completely. Overconfidence can cause risky assets. Private investors, who claim to be sure that the share is rising, take often a too large position in that stock. Through this overestimation of themselves they have made a decision that they would normally never take. But in investments nothing is sure. At any time can get a company into trouble. There are a lot of events that can ensure at any time of the day, you do not come true expectation. Sometimes you do this, but just as often expected does not come out. My point is not negative about the confidence of investors, but the facts are like that. I also have called out certain years, which shares would increase or decrease certain times. That did not always come off. Often there came after my announcement, events which I had absolutely no control over. I was delivered to news, which had a positive or negative effect on prices.

"Never be to sure about your thoughts"

In addition, often the thing happens that nobody expected. If anyone thinks that the stock market is going to rise, it will fall. And the opposite the same. Probably this is a reason. At the time, everyone thinks that the stock market will rise, these investors have already bought shares. Who will then provide an increase? Everyone looks at each other with the question: Hey, which buyers continue to buy? As investors, the media, and the banks are all positive about the stock market, then you'd better get out. An increase looks than too obvious. This means that all investors who would buy already bought. And there is no one left to care for a further increase.

"The unexpected always happens"

Vice versa. The moment all investors, banks and media are negative on the stock market or a particular stock, it is just a good time to buy the share. Anyone who wanted to sell, sold already. And the ground for an "unexpected" recovery seems often made. What would be expected, often not, and sure, therefore forgotten.

Too many times watching stock prices

In a world where you get at any time of the day from anywhere in the world internet at your disposal, it is very easy to follow the price of your shares. Is this just a great invention or this is just a risk for investors? Brokers do anything to particularly emphasize the advantages. They indicate, for example, that you're always on time when there is company news or if, for any reason, you want to sell shares. But why, if you're on the road or are at work or on vacation, you want to sell shares? Is it coincidence the right time to sell? And it is not so, then you're already too late if there is business news. Immediately after news, the share price reacts after already. So when you read the news on your mobile, it does not make sense anymore to respond to it. Of course, the share can be taken a certain direction, but the reaction to the news has been. Therefore, I think that keeping looking to stock prices, rather interferes with anywhere in the eye than it provides benefits.
Several studies have shown that frequent watching stock prices, has a strong influence on the emotions of investors. It causes investors to make decisions that they would otherwise not have taken. Keeping an eye on rates ensures that there will develop certain expectations

of its stock in your head. And subconsciously you will respond by selling or buying your share, which you are following. Both the fear of losing and the greed to miss out on profits, the reaction provoke to act.

"As long as your intention is not to sell your shares, keep on looking to your share price works simply prohibitive"

If you have a restrictive sense, it is time to take action. First, if you invest for the long term, it is not necessary to keep your eye on shares in the train on your mobile. You're not going to sell anyway, so why would you let yourself be influenced by fluctuating exchange rates? If you find that you are disappointed in the price trend this emotion can ensure that you sell in a mindless action your share via your mobile. While your goal was to invest for the long term. The more you look at the rates, the heavier it feels to invest. While investing is just as simple. Investing, and occasionally look in the newspaper to see how you're company is doing. It also appears that investors, who often look at the prices, much less appreciate the investment result. If you frequently look, the overall percentage change is much smaller than if you once a week, month or even look each quarter.

It is also good to walk away from your computer or you turn off your phone or tablet, if you find that stock prices have emotional impact on you. When I notice myself that I get emotional about my investments, because the result is disappointing or vertigo I get my share, I switch off my computer. I'm going to drink coffee or even walking outside a circle. If I then turn the computer back on, I realize I've lost that emotion. That kept me from making buy or sell decisions, which I would have otherwise made in my emotion. Investors may therefore not often look at the rates.

Fear and greed

One of the first stock exchange wisdoms you come across as an investor are the cries are *fear* and *greed*. Fear and greed are discussed for decades, but the most important emotions of investors. The fear of losing and the greed of always wanting more. Fear and greed are the greatest enemies of emotional investors and ensure that investors often do the opposite of how you should invest.
The fear of losing is high when the share falls. The loss increases and the more the stock drops, the greater the loss of the investor. The more the share drops, the sooner the investor wants to sell the share.

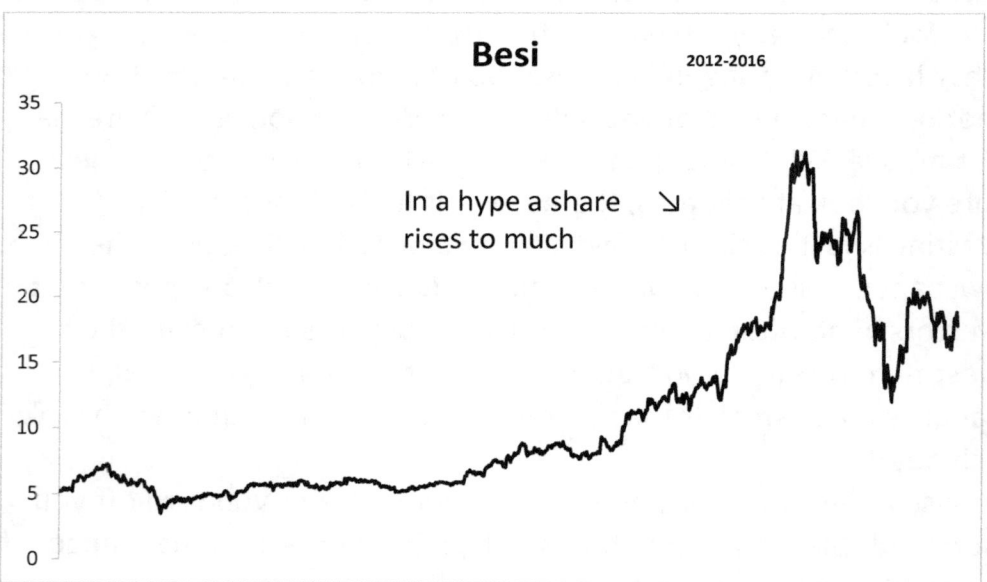

The greed of investors is increasing as a share rises. The trend is positive and investors see the trees grow into the sky. To take advantage of the rising share investors buy the stock or buy often more even if they already own the stock. However, they usually do this at the time, the hype has reached its peak.

It is apparent from the graphs above, that investors often do the opposite of the market movement. The fear of falling prices is often precisely the time to buy instead of sell. From greed would be wise just to sell shares instead of buying stocks that have risen far already.

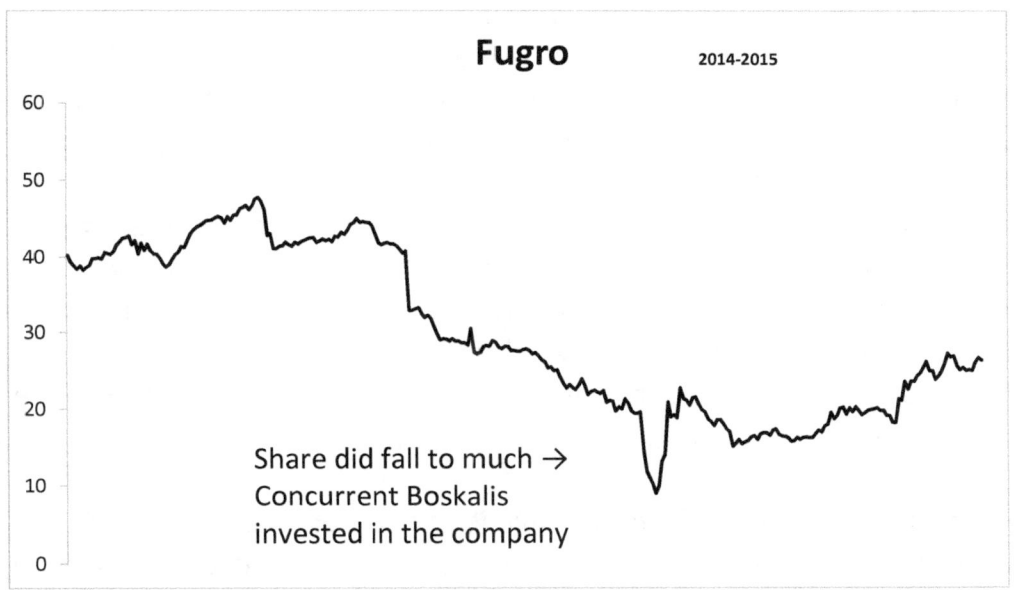

Investment alternative to savings

If the interest rate is low, it is not very attractive to put money in a savings account. This is useful in responding by providers of investment products. They play on the emotions of the people and let you move from a savings account to the stock market. And that is largely wrong.
People who save money in a savings account, have two possible targets. First to get some return on their savings and secondly to set money aside once or periodically to have money to do some big issue at some point.

"Saving and investing is comparing apples to oranges"

Savings interest rates bags already come in years and there seems as yet as no change. Over the years, the interest rate fluctuates violently. In 2008 it was at one time possible to receive 5% interest on a regular internet savings account. From that time the rate went down in a downward trend. Because savings due to low interest rates, according to experts *no point has* almost forced individuals to invest their savings. Based on performance, the experts are right. At a savings of 1% liver money in, if you subtract inflation and its load. Then choose the wise indeed for a different way of investing. But to direct individuals directly to the stock market is a bridge too far. On the stock price movements are a minimum of 1% per day rule rather than the exception. And savings gives you 1% per year. The risk of losing power on your savings account is up to € 100.000,- by the guarantee scheme - excluded. But the stock market, you can easily lose a part of your money every day. The risks of the stock market are so much greater, than compared to a savings account.

Another reason why individuals save is to keep on hand a certain amount as security to spend later to a particular purpose. Saving is not just for profit, but mainly to create certainty. For this reason, it is irresponsible to shift from a savings to the stock market.
Providers of investment products have the interest of themselves are paramount and see the importance of the saver overlooked. The investor would therefore not to leave by low interest rates tempt to invest. Saving is achieve more than just efficiency. But then a period lower interest rates, while remaining security.

Media

The media have great influence on the emotions of investors. People often turn to see the news from the media as fact, while these are only opinions. This is a common mistake. The media speak of the imperative and this has a major impact on the mindset of people. Newspapers can, by means of a large head, affect the whole stock market sentiment. It is precisely the media that ensure the sentiment on the stock market. And if possible, the media tries to be as negative as possible because bad news sells better once. Negative news sells because it is 'not normal'. The newspapers exaggerate events, resulting in a more negative trend. More negative than it should actually be. And people are greedier to read negative news. Good news is seen as normal, but bad news just excites people. People, and thus investors are simply conscious sensation. Newspapers are sold much better when the stock market falls, then when it rises.

We can conclude that the soup should not be eaten as hot as it is served. The negativity in the media is always a tad overdone. The stock market has recovered each time, for example after the real estate crisis, despite the big headlines in the media about the Greek, and China. When, based on this kind of reporting, you sell assets, you can repeatedly scratching their heads.

"Investors see the pronouncements of the media as facts, while these are only opinions of the writer"

Advertisements also have a negative impact on investors. There are many advertisements of investments and investor accounts that pull out all the stops to bind investors themselves. It now seems more to how much commission you pay on your investments, then the return on your investment. Known brokers do through commercials on TV and leaves everything to bind the customer to himself. The media devote too much attention to. Annually brokers even compared with the amount of the commission is important. In recent years, thousands of investors have switched to another broker. Sometimes on the basis of better service, more often has to make the transition to lower costs. Investors are guided too much by the smear campaign, which made the cost of the broker. The difference in cost is only a fraction of the overall performance of the investment portfolio. Of course, the investment result will be impacted by lower investment costs, but a slightly better timing of the purchase or sale of your shares has much more influence. Investors should therefore not attracting all advertisements of brokers, but focus more on the timing of their transactions. It pays much better results.

The market is not crazy

Sometimes it seems a share looks just very low or high. The question is: what is high and what is low? Many investors use the words high and low, but probably they mean undervalued and overvalued. High and low are only sentimental feelings of an investor. If a stock had been low, why should investors who own the stock, then sell their shares on the stock price? The stock is finally low. Are these investors accidentally stupid or find these investors that the share is not so low? The market is not crazy. High and low does not exist. Current stock prices are always right, but if you look to the future, you can judge for yourself whether you think that a stock has an up or down potential.

"The market is always right"

The stock market gives the right prices at any time. If prices had been low or high, there indeed was no trading in those shares. To create a rate, you need both a buyer and a seller. Watch out that you do not tell yourself that a share price is low or high. You have purely the expectation that based on the future, the share has upside or downside potential.

"High and low are only sentimental feelings of investors"

A good example is the stock ASML. The share price was in 2011 at € 25, -. In a straight line the stock rose the following years to € 65, -. According to many investors the share stood very high. Based on the increased share price it was indeed much higher than before. This does not mean that the share price was high or overvalued. Many investors decided at that time to sell the stock, as was the upward trend for a while in order. "From profit taking, no-one has become poorer" is a well-known adage. Taking profit is not bad, but to speak directly, the share price is too high, is not justified. Based on the earnings performance of the company ASML, the price increase was justified. Not for nothing, the share in the next two years rose further to over € 100, -.

'High' and 'low' are merely sentimental feelings from investors. Therefore, do not be convinced of your sentimental perception. Just look at the fundamentals.

High dividend

Beware of shares, which give a high dividend. It is not for nothing that the company gives a high dividend. Or rather, that the share price is so low so that the dividend is high. In the short term it seems very attractive to invest in stocks with a high dividend. Investors often declared that the dividend provides a floor for the share price. That is partly true, but investors forget that the risks are also higher for stocks with a high dividend.

A good example is the KPN share in 2011. The share was at a price of € 10, - and the dividend was at the rate of 10%. That is relatively very high and investors seemed to hit open goal. Who will soon know that investors would recoup their investment if they hold the share portfolio in ten years. The high dividend however was unsustainable and who had previously studied the company, would have known. KPN namely turned the vast majority of cash dividends and thus remained almost nothing about investing. This downward trend in the level of investment has long proved to be the case. The company was shrinking. Equally, we had a considerable debt, which is a thorn in the side end of each operation. KPN cut by the high dividend itself in the fingers and had to keep doing everything afloat. This share price dropped to € 2, - and the high dividend eventually proved a costly investment.

A high dividend you often see in companies and sectors that are under pressure. The oil and gas sector is the recent years, causing the share of hand Shell is done. At the current rate beginning in 2016 you can get a dividend yield of 9%. In this case, Shell has an excellent track record, but it's an omen that a record percentage is paid out in dividends. Investment forums asking investors are wondering how long this level Shell in an industry that is in decline, can maintain.

Also issued shares from the real estate sector are given often a high dividend yield. The ever-sinking rents for shops and offices, the financial position of these companies under pressure, which is reflected in falling stock prices. The high dividend should provide investors hold. The shopping and office goes back many years and the sector is therefore under pressure.

So be careful if you choose to invest in stocks with a high dividend. It is not for nothing that these shares are giving much dividend. Be aware that an investment in such shares entails many risks.

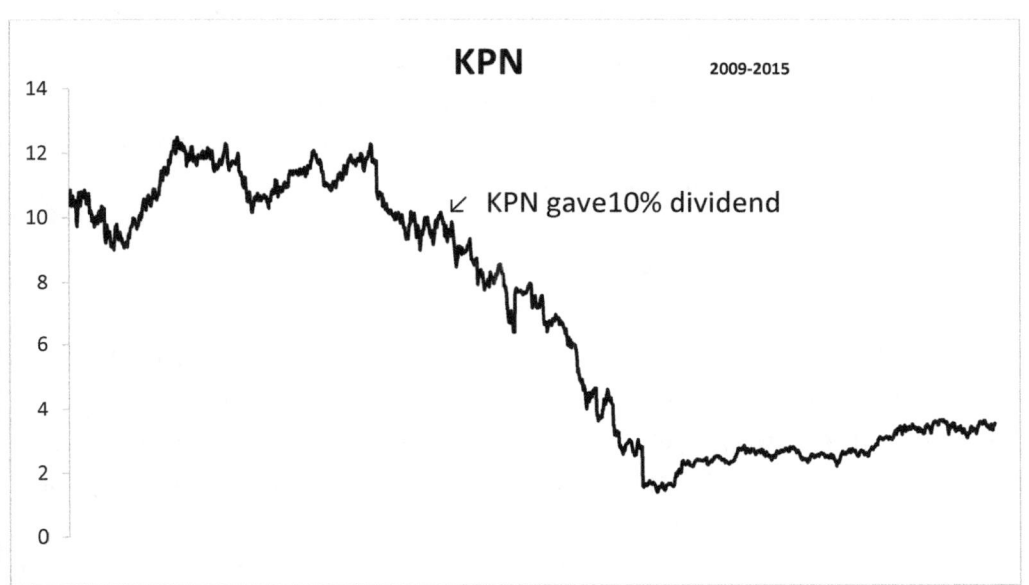

High speed trading

Try not to join the "big boys" in terms of the speed in stock trading. Financial parties have the best computers and systems and are always one step ahead of the private investor. Private investors run always respond several seconds behind events beyond equities. When economic numbers presented at 14.30 in the US economic data, the stock markets there almost always respond immediately. The parties of financial systems are adjusted so that each word or number, which is displayed in the presentation, enter a specific buy or sell. Private investors have a number of seconds or even longer to assess whether the economic data are a good thing or not, while financial parties have done the assessment within a few hundredths of a second. Do not try to compete in the speed of trading, because you win never as a private investor against a professional.

"Put your ego on the side and accept that some things you can better not better do"

In any case, I do not support it as a private investor as a day trader in shares. About 90% of the private day traders suffer from loss or stops too soon. It's the emotions of investors that make the day trader's career impossible. Therefore, do not try to make sure that you can. You may be the hero, which is possible, but the chance is nine times bigger that you are not.

Do not bet on just one share

My uncle taught me that the basic principle is that it is not smart to invest in a single share. It is not wise to be dependent on one company. If it's going fine, you making a lot of profit, but if it's not going well, your investment pleasure is soon over. By spreading you will prevent the dependence.

The reason for investing in a single share is often the lean investment budget. Mostly young people, who start investing, buy only one single share. Certainly if you are new to the investment world, the realization of risks is not yet optimal. After all, you have to walk to a pole to understand that you have to walk around it. You must take the consequences of risk, feel to understand what risk means. Each investor will make a profit and will lose sometimes. The longer you invest, the better you become. Even though no one can predict rates, your risk management, the main task of an investment adviser, has been greatly improved over the years.

I myself deal with a limit of € 1,000, - per share. The cost and the possible profit will only be interesting from that amount. To build a nice portfolio, you must have at least four different shares. From investable assets of around € 5,000 - is wise only to invest in stocks. That way you bring a nice spread and it's profitable. Depending on the risk you want to take, it is not necessary to include more than ten

different shares in your portfolio. However, it is wise to spread across multiple sectors, for example, not investing in both ING, ABN Amro and Delta Lloyd.
If you do not own € 5,000, - an ETF can offer you the solution. This way you spread your chances in a cheap way. There are many different ETFs, which will make everybody fit.

Advice from banks

Do not blame yourself for advice from banks. Analysts have different methods to get an opinion for a share. There are several figures that can be viewed. However, these are all figures from the past. Based on this, it is determined how the company will develop in the future. Not only for you, as a private investor, but also for analysts, the future is a mystery. You can have an expectation, but who says that expectations comes true? The future is unpredictable, and banks often have no idea which side will move a share. There are many factors that determine the stock prices. Any advice is outdated the day after. Every day there are new developments that can affect the prices or results of a company. Banks often follow the facts. Do not be blind to their opinions.

"Do not follow just the advice from banks"

Banks also have reasons in the advice they give. If a bank independently holds a large position in a company's share, the bank will often give a buy recommendation for that share. Sometimes banks are interested in the fact that a share increases or decreases. Those are those who play behind the scenes and are never brought out. There are very many dark transactions in the financial world, where the ordinary private individual does not know. Banks now have interests in certain price movements. An advice from a bank can not therefore be seen as an independent investment advice. When I started investing in the nineties, my buying and selling decisions were entirely dependent on the advice of banks. I considered analysts of banks as gods. After all, they had the knowledge to know which stocks you should buy and should not buy. At the time there was no internet yet and you could read your opinions only in newspapers, investment sheets and on teletext. At that time I decided to buy the Baan Company share. Several analysts indicated that the share could double. The share came from ƒ 10, - and was at the time I bought ƒ 80, -. That was the highest rate ever, but it would increase even further, according to analysts. The IT sector was currently *hot*. No analyst spoke about a hype. Banks advised massively to buy the share.

"Buy advice Baan Company Target Purpose ƒ 160, -"

At the moment that each bank gave a buying advice for Baan Company, the IT company collapsed. Even if all banks are positive about a share, that does not mean that the share is worth buying. Perhaps there were reasons to give a buying advice. In any case, it is wise never to make your purchase or sales decision subject to the advice of a bank. Follow your own thought, because as a self-employed investor you are the one who makes the decision.

Penny stocks

There are some disadvantages to an investment in the so-called penny stocks. As the name says, these shares are worth only a few pence. Actually all the shares, which belong under one euro, belong to the group of penny stocks. Firstly, you can wonder why these shares are worth so little. No share, which marks a few cents, does this because it is going so good with the company. In all cases, the share has been entered for a higher price. And so, all these companies have missed something, so the price has collapsed. An investment in a penny stock is therefore a big risk. It seldom happens that such a company flourishes again after a certain time like never before. There have been cases that this is true, but relatively, that chance is very small. If you invest in a penny stock, you should therefore take into account the risk of a large price loss or even a bankruptcy.

Secondly, the course of penny stocks is very erratic. They are often a playbook for speculators and private investors, who trade fast in and out to make a profit. There are seldom banks or professional institutions that follow penny stocks. Banks often handle the rule of law to follow only shares that are listed above the one euro. Speculators are therefore free to determine the price of the share. Not for nothing, these shares are often very popular on investment forums. Almost all members in these forums are private investors, so it's an excellent way to talk about penny stocks. Here, these shares are sometimes raised to cause a price response. Regular plans are made for everyone to buy a penny stock at the same time. This will then yield more buyers, which will increase the price. At the moment that all investors have entered, everyone wants to go through the same door again. The share is collapsing and the smart investors who started with have earned a lot of money. This phenomenon is called a *shuffle*.

"On investment forums, shuffles are prepared"

NewConomy's share was a popular playbook for many private investors at the beginning of this century. The share recorded in those years between € 0.05 and € 0.20. In forums investors were not excited about the share and several times a shuffle was set up. Similarly, in the summer of 2005. The share was already a time on a bid-offer price of € 0.07 to € 0.08. Below € 0.07 was a strong bottom, the share never dropped beyond that limit. It became more busy and busy on the IEX forum. You saw the amount of visitors that something was happening. Several investors at the NewConomy forum were talking about a possible stock plot of share in the coming days. Everyone was sharp, only you never knew if it would actually happen. Usually a shuffle starts immediately at the opening of the stock exchange in the morning. Similarly, that time with the

NewConomy share. The night before, investors made each other warm for the coming next day. The next morning, before the opening, the order book was already full of purchase orders at the lay price of € 0.08. With a large volume, the share opened at € 0.08 and with such an amount of shares, other speculators knew that many other investors would enter. With that thought, it was the fence of the dam and stepped into investors, without any faith in the NewConomy company, in the company's shares. The price movement is precisely determined by the investors, the so-called sheep of the investors who set up the shuffle. The share did not spell a minute later to € 0.09 and then note a few seconds later € 0.10. The shuffle lasted until the next morning, with the highest price on the bulletin board at € 0.14. Immediately afterwards everyone fell over and sold their shares. A few days later, the share returned € 0.07.

Winners and losers
Investors who start the shuffle: buy at € 0.08 and sell at € 0.13.
Investors who follow as a sheep to miss the boat: buy at € 0.13 and sell at € 0.07.

Shuffles are fun games to join, but it has nothing to do with serious investment. Because the majority of investors (the followers) eventually sold a loss, it took a few months to find new victims ready for a new shuffle.

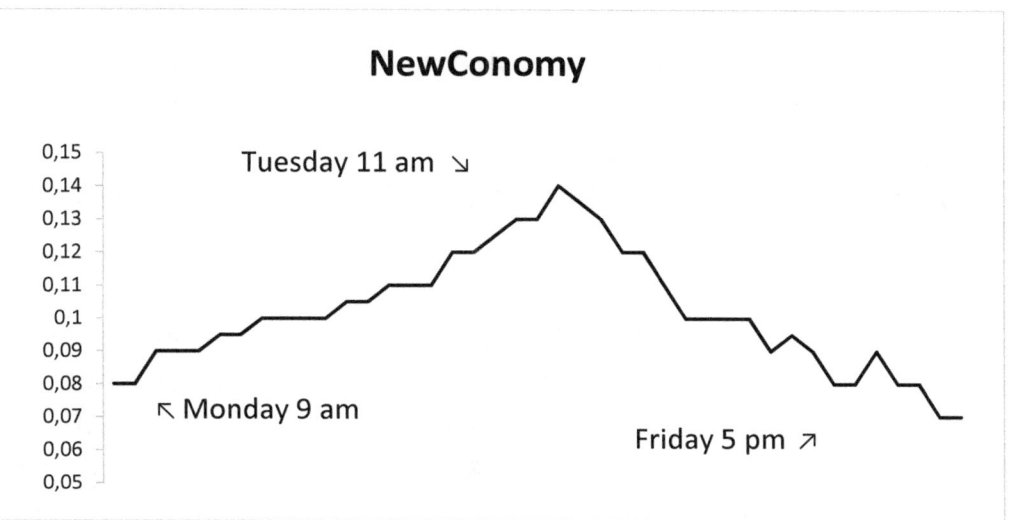

The crash

What investor is not afraid of a stock market crash? A stock exchange crash, which could drop the markets easily 30% in a single day. Striking is the fact that investors used to be much better off for a crash than today. A 30% crash in one day is no longer happening today, though it can never be ruled out. Nowadays you can speak of slumber crashes. These are crashes that do not occur in a single day, but are spread over several days and weeks in a row. Perhaps this change has to do with the fast information, accessible to all. Investors can therefore behave differently. A big crash rarely happens. From the archive it appears that there are tens or even hundred years between, before the next crash occurs.

Stock market crashes of the past took place in the year:

- 1773
- 1873
- 1882
- 1929
- 1987

In 2008 there was a slumber crash in global financial markets. The AEX fell in the respective first week of October with a 25%.

"In 2008, during the credit crisis, the AEX fell 25% in one week"

Crashes are caused by a flow of negative news, resulting in anxious investors, who sell at once. Other investors to follow the negative tendency, thus creating a snowball effect. The fear of negative news makes sure everyone is thinking negatively. If all investors think so at some point, everyone wants to sell and more. This caused the crash. My review shows that the market recovers and the situation finally was not as negative as expected. In a crash, it looks like investors are thinking the world goes down. Everyone sells his shares. Private investors take massive farewell to their shares. In a crash, investors no longer look at the fundamentals, but purely for the financial loss which is suffered on their stake. This means that investors make their decision based on emotions. And emotional decisions are almost never good at the stock exchange. At the time, the bags all the shares, you know it's not the fundamentals that lower stock prices, but the emotions of investors. Let your emotional never lead your marketing decision, but keep looking at the fundamentals.

Always want to have a position

Retail investors always have the urge to have an equity position. When investors have sold one position in shares should promptly bought another position. At least that's the idea. The money is simply aimlessly on the custody waiting for a new opportunity. And investors suggest that there are new opportunities every day. However, it is often better not to move too quickly into a new share. From emotion often investors take for a quick decision to buy one new share.

"No position is also a position"

Especially after profits made on the sold share. Then the investor is very sure about himself in the euphoria and he has the nerve to buy a risky stock to bluff the first success. On the other hand, after losing in the sold shares he takes just a stock with a high risk to thereby make it incurred losses as soon as possible. In conclusion, it can be suggested that investors because of their positive or negative emotion take uncontrolled risks without fundamentally there long enough to have thought about it. Therefore, it is often better to wait a little longer to making your next purchase. I myself sleep nowadays overnight, after I sold a position. The emotion is the next day, tumbling back pocket, you can make basically a good choice. I also notice that you pay attention better at the appropriate entry level after a break. By not reckless directly to step in, you can just quietly waiting for the right entry level. It is difficult to determine the appropriate entry level, but take as a guide the share price at which you buy the shares worthy.

Therefore, be not too keen when you have a sale of your shares, investment funds again, but sleep there first night on, so you do not emotional, a new purchase. Often you come to new insights.

Alternative investments

Besides the market there are other ways to invest. For example, you also invest in ships, teak, art, unlisted bonds and movies. The disadvantage compared to investing in the stock market is that these investments are often not easy to sell. In most cases, you sit there for months or years to determine. On the one hand well, so you are not guided by emotions, may sell quickly, but at the same time it's a big risk. If you have suddenly need the money or is it suddenly a bad investment, you walk behind the facts.

When you invest in shares, often in companies, which for many years or even decades of existence. The providers of alternative investments are often new or still have no track record. This creates a greater risk because the provider has not yet or not sufficiently proven. They are often smaller companies, which are also much faster to fall.

You'll recognize determine the commercials on TV and the internet. You can invest in unlisted bonds, where you can earn 8% per annum. And at the end you get your money back, hopefully.... Or an investment in vessels with a yield of 12%. A film fund which you can earn as much as 24%. A property fund with 10% efficiency and have a shot at the value of the underlying asset. Or investing in wine? These are just some examples where good returns are promised, which are often less beautiful in reality. At times, the savings rate is low, it is an excellent time to entice individuals with sample returns for suppliers of these products.

I myself participated once in alternative investments by stepping into a bond of Centurion. Centurion invested the money in recreational real estate in Costa Rica, a country that was on the rise, according to them. And therefore just a good investment. The company started in 2009. So I took part in the first issue of bonds. Later there followed more issues. I was tempted by the fixed return of 8.4% and invested € 10.000, -. As a result, I received € 70, - per month and would return my deposit received at the end of the term. It went well and so good that I got my deposit before return. That's what I got a bonus yield of 3%. The total investment in the Centurion bond was three years instead of five years and ended up being quite a success.

A few years later Centurion went bankrupt. The prosecution blames the bankruptcy fraud by the directors of the company. They have been in custody in jail. In retrospect, I'm glad I was not once joined a bond of Centurion. The people who have done so have now been (partly) lost their money. Of the two founders of Centurion indeed due to any fraud, I highly doubt. I rather think that the situation has robbed the drivers. In any case, the end exercise for Centurion. And, the risk of investing in a start-up painful. Small startup companies often go bankrupt and the beautiful return of 8.4%, which investors are attracted, by then even to mention the large low risk.

Several financial experts put their questioning alternative investments. In newspapers and on the Internet a lot to find their opinion on various products. Often these types of investments are extremely risky and sample returns are too good to be true. Not everything is bad, but try to find the golden eggs. So be very careful when doing alternative investments.

5. What you better should do

After a series of examples of how you should better not invest, it is now time for examples of how to better invest.
Investors emotions ensure that you make mistakes, as described in the previous chapter. And it is important to avoid this. In the examples I emphasize two things. Avoiding short-term trading to increase your winning chances and risks decrease, making you keep control of your emotions investors.

Buying long term call options

Seen over a longer period, shares always rise. It is not a certainty, but the opportunity is huge. With that mindset, you can achieve a higher price gains by buying long-term call options. The longer the term of the option, long-term call options are getting cheaper. Many investors often choose to buy just short-term options. Which finally appear cheaper, while relatively speaking is not. As mentioned earlier, running about 75% of the options worthless. The majority of these are short-term options. The probability that a given percentage increase in the span of a month, is much smaller than on the basis of a period of three years for example. Short term options can be realized a huge profit, but long-term options, this is certainly the case. Only you have, because of the longer period simply have a little more patience.
Volatility and price expectations determines the value and therefore the attractiveness of the call option. Not long-term options are issued to all shares. It is mainly the large stocks in the AEX, which already recorded a time in the index. You can think of Aegon, ING, Shell and Unilever.
It is often wise to buy out of the money call options. Relatively speaking, the attractiveness less than or at the money calls. If you're expecting a very large price increase of a share can out of the money options are attractive percentage. However, the chance that this will be the case, is a lot smaller.

Example:
The current price of ING at time of writing is € 13.45.
Relatively speaking, the call option in December 2019 with a strike price of € 12, - is an attractive option.
The price of this is € 2.70.
The net asset value is € 1.45 (€ 13.45 - € 12, -), so the time / expectation comes out at € 1.25.
ING shares in December 2019 should therefore be at least € 14.70 for profit. That is at the time of writing a term of four years. The likelihood that ING interim or on the expiration date of the option is many times higher, is very large.

Example situation in December 2019:

- Share ING stands at € 10 , - . It's bad with the economy and thereby share ING collapsed. The final value of the option is thus € 0, - . You've lost everything.
- Share ING stands at € 15 , - . The call option expires on
€ 3, - (€ 15,- minus € 12,-) and you have a profit earned from € 0.30 million (€ 3,- minus € 2,70)
- Share ING stands at € 25,- The call option expires at € 13,- (€ 25,- minus € 12 , -) . You have a profit of € 10.30 (€ 13 - - € 2.70)

In the last example, you could take the shares have achieved an efficiency of 85%. With the call option you had booked a return of 455%.

Writing call options

The opposite of buying options is writing options. You play the opponent of the person who buys the option. Since about 75% of options expire worthless, it is clear what investor will earn the most; the writer off the option. When 75% of the buyers are the options with loss, this means that 75% of the writers of options profits. The stock market adage is not without reason: Who writes that bites.

"Who writes that bites'

It is possible to write calls and puts. And writing calls it advisable to do so on the shares you already own. This is called "covered writing." Puts you can write not covered. With a call option you have the possibility to buy shares at a pre-agreed price. By written calls you have the obligation to sell shares at a pre-agreed price, provided it is of interest to the buyer of the option, of course. Because the writing covered options are more attractive and less risky, I keep only writing about call options in this chapter. Below is an example of writing calls on stocks.

Example:
You own 200 shares in Shell. This you bought for € 23, on November 1, 2015 -. The current price is € 23.35. You decide to write calls on November 17, 2015 call options on your shares. It is wise to write calls that are at the money or out of the money. The point is that you earn at the time / expected value of the option and not the intrinsic value. The intrinsic value of the option will be paid namely by yourself. The example below makes this clear.
Opening Sale 2 (= 200 shares) calls in December 2015
€ 23.50 for € 0.65
You will receive 2 x € 0.65 = € 130, - (200 shares)
Situation on expiry in December 2015 of call options:

- Shell price € 22,- , you keep your shares, but you earned € 130,- by receiving the premium, on the other hand are the shares now below your purchase price, thus you have a foreign exchange loss on your shares.
- Share Shell € 23.50 , you keep your shares and also have € 130,- earned the premium received.

- *Shell price € 25,- , the shares you have to deliver at € 23.50 each. You have € 130,- earned. However, you loose € 1.50 euros per share, because your shares are higher then € 23.50 . Along with the premium you end recharged price is € 23.50 + € 0.65 = € 24.15. You had a total of € 0.85 per Share you could get more if you had not written the calls.*

Whether the proportion is higher or lower than the price at which you write the options, you know you at least € 130, - have earned, whatever happens. That amount can not be removed. You're sure of that profit. The maximum you could earn your position (200 shares + 2 written call options) was a retail price of € 24.15. Only afterwards will show whether this was attractive. However, no one knows in advance what rate is the share on the date of the expiration. You click to set you profits on the share, and then you get paid by the option premium received.

Additionally contain short-term calls proportionately more time / expectation over the long term calls. It is therefore advisable to prescribe short-term calls. Instead of once a year to write a call option, you better write twelve times a month call option. The final sum is much more attractive for the investor who writes calls, because the outcome is higher.

"Write short and buy long"

Many investors ignore this extra income. People find it boring, because you know in advance your maximum profit from your stock position. In addition, the majority of people find an option strategy too hard and therefore do not burn their fingers. However, the writing of options is much easier than people think. Also, you often hear people call that the premium that you receive as a writer of options, is not very much. But that's not true. On an annual basis this is a very big part of your eventual profit. And finally, people are afraid, they have to deliver their shares when the price is higher than the strike price. People need to realize that you can buy back the shares again. There is nothing special about and thereby prejudices can be put in the refrigerator.

Call spread

Another interesting possibility is a combination of buying a call option and writing a call option. This option strategy limits the earnings of the purchased call option, but it makes you to do a lower investment. There are investors who apply this strategy by default. Yet this interesting possibility remains underestimated by many investors. Perhaps investors believe that this strategy is difficult. This strategy is much easier than many think.
A call spread you buy a call option to then sell a call option with a higher strike (strike price) at the same time. With many brokers you can give the order at once. You do not have an order for both buying and writing separately to pass. This strategy is attractive when you expect increases an index or share limited. You expect a rise but no price explosion.

For example, you expect the AEX will rise, but do not expect very big price explosion. The current state of the AEX 472 points in November 2015. You expect the AEX in a period of about a month will rise to 490 points.
Buy AEX call 470 in December at a price of € 10.50.
Write AEX call 490 in December at a price of € 2.60.
You pay € 7.90 (€ 10.50 and € 2.60 to receive payment)
Two sample situations:

       1. The AEX rise in December to 485 points
Price call option in December 470 closing at € 15.00 million (€ 485 - € 470, -)
Your investment was € 10.50.
Additionally, you receive € 2.60 EUR for the written call option.
Your profit is € 7.10.

If you had bought only call option in December 470, your profit was € 4.50 (€ 15,- minus
€ 10.50).

2. The AEX rise in December to 500 points

The AEX increased more than 490 points at which you wrote the call option. Your profit is limited to 490 points. You miss in a price of 500 points 10 points. However, you do receive € 2.60 for the written call option. You miss net € 7.40.
However, you still achieved a very nice profit:
Sales profit of 470 call option in December was € 9.50
(€ 490, - - € 470, - = € 20, - - € 10.50)
Additionally, you receive € 2.60 for the written call option.
Your total profit is € 12.10.

Example 1 shows a call spread is more profitable than buying only a call option. The fact that the AEX closes no higher than the written call option ensures that you do not miss out profits. In addition, you have taken advantage of the option premium you received it.
From Example 2 shows that the AEX closes higher than the written call option. In this case, you had, in retrospect, better not buy a call spread. Namely you're missing some of the profits. However, there is none of this in advance sure. The lost profit is mitigated by the price, you receive from the written option.

Stop losses and run profits

As mentioned in the book under the topic "what you better not do" is written, it is important losses on positions to cut off in equities and let profits run. But that sounds logical and easier than imagined. From a psychological standpoint, investors are just inclined to do the opposite. The vast majority of private investors makes that mistake. Professional investors doesn't make that mistake because they do not act emotionally. The failure of private investors is that they are too much guided by their emotions. It is therefore important to keep your emotions in control.

One way to stay on top of your emotions, by presetting your price limits. For example, you can set a stop loss on your stock position. If you previously set up how much you want / can lose on your position, you actually doesn't need any longer to look at the prices. Often people keep prices in order to check how much money they earn or to check if their investment turns out negative. If you know in advance how much you want to lose as a maximum, the last reason is no longer an option. You must first determine how much you could lose up to your position. It is prudent to provide for per share. One share is now once more volatile and risky than the other. If you still want to determine an average stop-loss, 10% would be a common percentage. It saves a person what he finds convenient, but you can catch a bad time of a share of 10% and exceed you, for me, not the maximum allowed. When you have this set up, you can concentrate fully on the odds of the stock.

You could also set a limit, when the proportion of a certain profit is to sell the share. And that limit can obviously set higher than the stop-loss percentage, you just set. For example, you may decide to set a limit of 30% profit. If you set a stop-loss as well as a limit for profit, it is actually not necessary to follow the share prices. Before is already clear your profit or loss, so the surprise is much less. This way of investment ensures that you will look fewer times to stock prices and makes you not act emotionally. An event, which raised a stock quote or reduced, ultimately does not affect your investment decision, because you've already determined ahead of your limits. Additionally, you can enjoy the interim dividend, you may receive.

"Stop losses and run profits, is only possible if you have your emotions in check"

If you're completely in control of your emotions, it is not necessary to pre-set limits. However, I know from experience that by far the majority of retail investors are not the boss over their emotions. They will not, however, admit it and that is why so many private investors so often bump the same stone.

Investing regularly

When is the perfect time to buy stocks? The question many investors will ask themselves and others. The trouble is that nobody knows the answer to that question. There are plenty of people who have an opinion on when that perfect moment occurs. But surveys show that as many of those people have the right or wrong. There is no foolproof system to determine when the right time buying and selling of shares is. To avoid having to gamble, it is wise to regularly buy or sell shares. That way you take advantage of the one time of a favorable exchange rate, but other times you're out of luck. Those moments are balanced. If you do this a few years maintains a row, the chances of winning are very high. Based on several years has, on average, an equity investment namely always profitable. The main stages in boarding, is that the prices at the moment you want to sell, are higher than when you bought them. Interim is a drop just attractive, because you can get in cheaper. It also depends on your investment term or phased boarding is advisable. There is no limit on which phased boarding or is inadvisable. Still, I think you at least pull out a five-year term, you want to limit the risks of boarding stages. The probability of return is such a term also greater, because you can get in cheaper. It also depends on your investment term or phased boarding is advisable.

"With phased entry and exit you control your emotion"

Another advantage of this technique is that you turn off your emotions as an investor. Emotion is the greatest enemy of the private investor. If you already know in advance when you turn on or get off, you do not prematurely make emotional decisions. And any emotional decision you avoid, has a positive effect on your final return.

In addition to a phased boarding, it is also possible to phased to step out. This depends on the purpose for which you want to sell. Do you need a certain amount each month, you can do this through the proceeds of your sale staged. If, on the basis of not wanting to gamble at the right price selling, phased want to get off, which is also possible.

Trading signals

There are several providers of systems indicating trade signals for the purchase and sale of shares, options or other financial instruments. If you do not have the time or knowledge to make decisions, this can be a godsend. Another advantage is that you do not have emotion, you influenced in making investment decisions. You leave work and taking the decisions by actually doing another. All you have to do, is to give the order to your broker. With some providers it is even possible to directly send it to your broke, so you have to do anything yourself.
Obviously it costs money to receive the advice service and in addition you should also look closely at the performance of the service. It would be too easy to think that this kind of providers can offer a certain return. However, the advantage of knowledgeable people behind this advisory, which increases the chance of a good return. When you purchase a service like this, you usually get an annual subscription and is annual or monthly subscription money from your account debited. The advisory service sends you an SMS, WhatsApp message or an e-mail at the time the provider sees an opportunity to buy a stock or sell. You must then decide yourself whether you join it by entering an order with your broker. As mentioned earlier, it is possible for some providers to automatically convert the advice to order.
When you decide to purchase such advisory, it is advisable to look at the past results. Although past performance is no guarantee for the future, this is a way to see what you could expect. It is also advisable

to get involved with a not too small amount to this, because the potential benefits have to outweigh the cost of the consultancy.

ETF

An ETF is recommended, as you with little money still want to build a diversified investment portfolio. An ETF invests in a fixed basket of shares. You can think of an ETF on the AEX, which invests in all twenty-five shares of the AEX. Besides indices are also ETFs sectors, regions, commodities, currencies and precious metals. The aim of an ETF is to track as closely as possible the underlying. An ETF on the AEX index will seek to follow the direction of the index.

"ETFs are very useful when you are with little money still want to spread your risk"

ETFs are also sometimes compared to mutual funds. That is partly justified. The difference is that the fund manager of an investment fund aims to put out a performance. His goal is to book the best return relative to its competitors in the sector. An ETF will not out perform and aims to make it as good or bad as an index or any of the other underlying is performing.

Managing an investment fund takes more time, and thus more money, than an ETF. The publisher of an ETF finally do not have to think how he needs to invest. This makes ETFs much cheaper than mutual funds. Because managers of investment funds in the majority of cases do not perform better than the market average is not paying for this money wisely.

If you do not have too much money, which you want to invest, it is highly recommended to opt for an ETF. The limited costs can thus have a broad portfolio selected.

Each year a dip

Investors are always looking for the right time buying and selling of their shares. However, it turns out only later if the time was correct or not. The opposite of what investors think, happens often. And it is wise to act properly upon it called contrarian investing.

"The investor behavior ensures that contrarian investing is profitable"

Literally every year there comes a time when prices sharply lower. Sometimes it seems like everything goes well at the stock exchange. Shares rise due to economic growth, improved by operating results and a low interest rate. Banks give a buying advice for almost all of the shares and the trees seem to grow up into the sky. Just then it is wise to be vigilant. The transition can sometimes be faster than investors think. It is much wiser to take profits just when it is going well at the stock exchange. Then finally few investors who want to sell shares, making stock prices are high. So do the opposite of what the co-investors. At a time of increasingly negative reports and falling prices, it is often time to buy stocks. That's contrarian investing. Beginning in 2015, the stock markets experienced a period of growth and the AEX rose within four months from 400 points to 500 points. The global economy was growing and the interest rates was increasingly under pressure. Under the slogan TINA (There Is No Alternative) private investors invested all their money in stocks. Finally was then tapped the 500-point threshold. An increase in the AEX of 25% in four months is, moreover, quite large. The question is whether it is to justify such a large increase. Banks and other investment gurus came up with positive stories, the AEX was going to rise to 600 points. After all, there was no noticeable negative message, so why the AEX should drop? The economy is very good and it would only get better. However, I can tell you that there really any year, a dip in the stock market is happening. At the time, banks and investors are so positive about equities, there is indeed no reason to be negative. However, you should look forward as an investor. Is it about a month, three months or a year still as good as now? For why should it be necessarily not to continue positive? At the time the AEX made a great rise and everyone remains positive, this is often a sign of greed. Just after an increase investors would AEX 25% to scratch their heads: Why the AEX should rise further? Is economic growth of 1.5% reason to celebrate this so exuberant? Three months or a year still as good as now?

After the AEX quails remained about three months around a stand of 500 points, negative news prevailed. The Chinese economy grew more slowly than expected. That caused the AEX fell in August to 400 points. Surprisingly, this was not. Surprisingly, however, in the sense that China was concerned, but not surprising that there was negative news. Each year the fair has both positive and negative messages. The fact that investors properly alighted masse at an AEX-state of 400 points is the typical behavior of investors. Chinese shrinkage would actually ensure that Dutch companies would be severely affected and that justified an AEX 300 to 350 points. A few months earlier the AEX would rise from 500 to 600 points, and now suddenly expectations drops from 400 to 300 points. This exaggeration will always be there and you just respond on it. At the time, investors want to sell all at AEX 400, you should buy shares. That's contrarian investing. Buy when everyone is negative and just sell when everyone is positive.
I compare the fair ever with the human health. In the summer someone feels for example very healthy, fit, energetic, athletic and thinking it is on top of the world. At that point you can not think of a cold or you may get anything. You are then resin complication positive. Yet almost everyone gets the flu once a year. For example if the autumn starts, people start sniffling and if any adversity, you lie with the flu a week in bed. At that moment, you feel bad, without energy, negative and miserable. You did not think the summer ahead, you'd be far, so bad. You are super negative. And that would be in terms of shares just be the time to buy stocks. Because you know you are, anyway, again recovers from the flu, although you there are still

totally unaware of at the time. After sunshine follows rain, and after rain follows sunshine.

"ING Investment Barometer contra indicator"

A good indicator to measure investor sentiment, is the ING Investment Barometer. ING assesses monthly investor confidence. The greater optimism and confidence, the higher the position of the barometer. The AEX is therefore almost always on a high setting. If the confidence is low, it appears that from a low position of the barometer. The AEX is nearly always lower than before. To act contrarian, you can use the ING investment barometer, to buy at low setting shares and sell shares at a high position. This will take advantage of the emotional pitfalls of other investors.

Crisis

An economic crisis is causing plummeting stock markets. However, it appears that every crisis is only temporary and always restore the financial markets. If we look at the last twenty years, Beursplein 5 Amsterdam has many crises behind.
In 1997 there was the Asian crisis. This crisis began much too exuberant life in many Asian countries. The growth was huge and there were many billions from around the world to invest in Asian countries, because the economy was booming. It turned out that the growth was too fast, causing the bubble burst. The starting point was when Thailand decided its currency, the baht to devaluate. That led to a collapse of the baht by more than 50%, whereby debts were unsustainable. The crisis in Thailand soon expanded to other Asian countries and so came the Asian crisis. The result was mass layoffs and poverty. The crisis was so great that even Russia, America, Brazil and Europe suffered the consequences. This is because these economies are dependent on each other. The AEX decreased by 24% during that period.

A direct consequence of the Asian crisis, the Russian financial crisis in the summer of 1998, also known as the Ruble crisis. By the Asian financial crisis and the fall in prices of raw materials, the demand for the ruble fell. The Russian government wanted to keep the price artificially high, and had to borrow foreign capital. However, this was not sustainable and in August 1998 the bomb burst. The stock market crashed in Moscow and the ruble lost much of its value. Worldwide went shockwaves across the exchanges and Amsterdam went prices for July - October 1998 with 39% down.

A few years later, in 2001, the Internet bubble followed. In 1996, the big business it became clear that *the worldwide web* unparalleled commercial opportunities had in themselves and that it was there full on target. These capabilities were soon seen by smart, young people and thus made the beginning of *the new economy* . Internet companies shot up like mushrooms from the ground. Investors played only too happy to these unprecedented opportunities. Then also boarded the private investor, the Internet bubble was, by irrational expectations of the market completely inflated. When it appeared that the results of many companies, due to a surplus of this type of business, were disappointing, the bubble was empty. Stock prices, which had risen too hard, caused a slumber crash on stock markets worldwide. The AEX declined during this period by more than 60%.

In 2007 came the credit crisis, which has lasted more than a year. This crisis started in America, because housing prices there, after a long period of growth, stagnated. Partly because bonds with mortgages as collateral worth less quickly. Then came financial institutions in trouble and was written for hundreds of billions by banks purchased bonds. It was unclear exactly which institutions would be in trouble, hence the interbank money nobody dared each other to lend and dried up. Banks borrowed even not a penny to each other. Several banks collapsed and were nationalized. The AEX decreased by 55% during that period.

"It always comes back well after an economic crisis, the stakes are simply too big now"

If we look at the above list of crises over the last twenty years, you can conclude that each crisis has to do with overinflated economic system. It also appears that after each crisis the economy recovers and stock markets rebounding. The importance of keeping intact the global economic system, once very big now. Governments and central banks often jump during a crisis to support markets. Although the majority of investors are selling shares in a crisis, it's just not wise to do this or even buy in. It is important to look at what is kind of crisis and which stocks you can buy the best. During the Internet bubble all the shares fell, while mainly the internet and tech companies were the culprits. So why a declining share as Ahold or Shell declining extremely hard? And the same goes for the financial crisis of 2007. What have Ahold and Shell with the credit crisis. In a crisis sinks complete confidence and the entire economy, including Ahold and Shell, those brands. However, these ticks are much smaller and such companies recover much faster. It is often advisable to buy decent share in the crisis. Even if it takes a year or longer, the probability of return is very high. And when everyone is excited again about the economy, you can resell such shares.

Solid companies

It is wise to invest at least half of your investment portfolio in solid companies. And with that I mean companies that have proven themselves over many years. These companies can usually take a crisis. The longer a company exist, the more stable the company usually is. Good examples of stable companies are ING, Royal Dutch Shell, Ahold, ASML, DSM, Wolters Kluwer, Randstad and Heineken. Often these companies give such a stable dividend.

"Boring investing is investing well"

The opposite of solid companies are the companies that operate primarily driven sentiment. Companies that are quick coming up, can also just disappear quickly into the abyss. These are also companies that take risks by, for example explosive growth by making acquisitions. Or companies that make a lot of debt to make acquisitions. Characteristics of non-solid companies are strong fluctuations in the company's turnover and operating profit / loss. Internet companies such as World Online, quickly became successful, but disappeared just as quickly the radar. Companies in the 3D sector shot up like mushrooms from the ground. Those shares were running, but the majority is hard again collapsed. Those companies are not completely solid, you have no idea what to think about it. It is not wrong to invest in such sectors, but because they are not strong, the risk is very big. Invest therefore only a minimal part of your ability.

Companies active in the biotechnology shot up like mushrooms from the ground. There is a huge hype arise and these shares have a considerable appreciation. If at least half of your investment portfolio consists of solid companies will give you more confidence and therefore less stress, so you can keep your investors emotions under control. And these shares can, as previously named, for example, writing calls to ensure that additional income. Together with the dividend that you receive makes annually for a decent income. The smaller portion of your investment portfolio, you can then invest as stocks, where more stress is coming from.

Invest in companies with rising dividends

As described in the previous chapter, you should be wary of companies that pay high dividends. History has proven that it usually dangerous investments. It is much better to invest in stocks with increasing dividends. These are not high dividend stocks, but stocks with a good track record. Those shares are solid, because back confidence built up over the years. Such a company will not just go cut the dividend. Firstly, the revenue model of the relevant company is adjusted so that a rising dividend can be maintained. Second, the company wants to not disturb his track record, because the long-established reputation directly to tarnish.

"Stocks with rising dividends show a much better performance than stocks with only a high dividend"

The good thing about stocks with increasing dividends is that they show a much better performance in the long term than stocks with a stable, high dividend. They are growth stocks and that class of shares, investors pay a higher rating, which translates into an annual rising share price. Stocks with high dividend are not. Companies spend just a high dividend, because they can only make investors happy by that way. Real estate companies have this kind of difficult to increase profits and sales. *High dividend investors* are often investors, which in the short term to earn as much money. And that does not always.

Use common sense

Do not just rely on what advisors, gurus or fellow investors tell you. Also use your own mind. Step only in a particular stock or a particular investment if you believe in it completely. Of course, you never know for sure whether a stock rises or how much return you will make. Make sure that you have that expectation and that you understand which you invest in. If you already have question marks at the start of an investment return opportunities you can better not buy the stock. Do believe what you invest in, what are the potential profit opportunities and risks associated with this investment. Look around you. What is happening around you, is the economy. You see as a private person first which trends and hypes are coming. You notice for example that your family, friends or bystanders are increasingly interested to purchase a mobile phone? Buy a stake in the telecom industry! See that attracts the labor market? Then buy a share of the broadcasting sector! You read that more and more private investors are investing in the Netherlands? Buy a broker like BinckBank. Turns out there are still more letters sent than previously thought? Buy PostNL. You will first see what happens, then it is only the media and the markets that follow. Read newspapers, websites and follow current affairs programs on emerging trends. What you see is the real economy, and you can act on it as an investor by buying these shares.

Spread you portfolio

Proper diversification reduces risk and therefore fewer emotions among investors. You sleep as an investor then finally a lot better. As mentioned earlier, it is not recommended investing in a single share. Although many (beginning) investors have limited investment capacity, it is often inevitable to invest in one or two stocks. It is better to invest in an ETF. From € 5.000, - you can build a portfolio with four different stocks. The more power, the easier it is to build a nice portfolio. It is not advisable, if you have less than € 50,000, - to invest, to build a portfolio of 100 different names. That is completely unnecessary and administratively too clumsy. A breakdown in ten different stocks is enough, provided you mainly arranges your portfolio with solid stocks. And if you have ten shares also spread over different countries and sectors, it is, in terms of distribution of opportunities and risks, perfect. If you have more to invest than € 50.000, -, then it is advisable to invest in more than ten different stocks.

Boring investments are good, but investors often want more excitement. It is therefore wise for example to invest 80% in equities and to invest 20% in somewhat speculative. That way you make sure that you still keep it stress less, while by far the most of your investments are in decent stocks. Below is an example of how a well-diversified investment portfolio can look like. In addition, I use three different amounts.

A € 1000, -

- € 1000, - ETF AEX index

Despite € 1.000, - is a small amount to invest with, you can buy through an ETF and choose a wide spread.

B € 5000, -

- € 1. 250 - Royal Dutch Shell shares
- € 1. 250 - shares Sanofi
- € 1. 250 - KBC Bank shares
- € 1. 250 - shares Wolters Kluwer

From € 5.000, - on you can start building a portfolio of individual shares. Of course you can choose the shares, but in this example I created a variety of sectors and countries. You could also choose to replace one instance or more shares for ETFs.

C € 50.000, -

- € 5 . 000 - shares ING
- € 5 . 000 - shares Apple
- € 5 . 000 - shares Total
- € 5 . 000 - shares Adecco
- € 5 . 000 - shares Wereldhave
- € 4 . 000 - shares Porsche
- € 4 . 000 - Shares Walmart
- € 4 . 000 - shares Gilead Pharmaceuticals
- € 3 . 000 - shares Sanofi
- € 2 . 000 - turbo long Randstad
- € 2 . 000 - Long-term call option DSM
- € 3 . 000, - ETF long Silver
- € 3 . 000, - ETF long Emerging Markets

In this example I used a considerable variation. You can see sound companies from different countries and sectors. By far the majority, or 80%, has been invested in shares. 20% I chose a combination of ETFs and long term call options. In addition, I opt for even more variety by also adding a precious metal. On the shares ING you can also write monthly short call options to generate extra returns.
The above investments are merely examples of how a well-diversified portfolio might look like. You can change the companies obviously yourself.

One-time setback

Sometimes, businesses are faced with a major setback, which has a large negative impact. As a result the share price falls significantly. When such a setback is disposable, it may be wise to buy those shares. A single setback only have a negative impact on the operating result in that year. Of course, the image damage can result if there are still some additional costs or problems the following year. But that will be limited, often turns out. When a single setback does not affect the business, it is just wise to buy the shares and put them away for a few years. Chances are very high that the stocks are then recovered.

"A one-time setback is an excellent buying opportunity"

A good example is oil company BP. The oil spill in the Gulf of Mexico caused major damage. On April 20, 2010 there was an explosion on the oil rig of BP and it eventually sank. This allows the drill rod and leaked three months, oil broke into the sea. BP was found guilty justice for this terrible natural disaster. The correct decision resulted in a cost of many billions. The share price of BP, listed on the London Stock Exchange, fell from 650
pence to 300 pence. This halving of the share price made it directly into an excellent buying opportunity. The disaster in the Gulf of Mexico was an incident, so a single setback.

BP's earnings was obviously just the same, and therefore the company could simply record the following year old earnings. Thereby also hear the old share price of around 650 pence. A year later the shares were trading at 550 pence again.

Setbacks provide a falling stock price. When a setback is an incident, it may be a good time to pick up the shares at the lower share price. Once the business model is not affected, you can speak of a single setback. Be certain that the setback is single and has no impact on the earnings of the company in the future.

Patience is a virtue

Investing means investing for the longer term. You invest in the company, because you have the expectation that the share price is attractive by certain developments. This increases the share price. However, your expectation is not always immediately. You think the share, for example, in about half a year, will be higher than now. It does not always happen in the short term what you expect. Sometimes it simply takes longer before the hidden value of the share emerges. Have patience. If you believe in your investment, you can keep the share better longer than the more direct selling, because you are tired of waiting for good results.

"The biotech sector requires the most patience"

A sector where your patience is tested, is the biotech sector. A biotech company may have spent years researching and testing, without even receiving a penny. Moreover, growing long each idea into a product. Rarely comes after years of studies and tests actually a drug to market. There should be clear phases are completed before a drug can be sold. Investors obviously hope that the company successfully bringing a drug to market what is a blockbuster. Until there is positive news comes from a biotech company, the share price usually stays flat or moves slowly downward. This is because the money runs out. The company has only costs and there is no money inside. Therefore, the probability increases that should be collected through the issue of new money. This causes a downward course. Sometimes pharmacists' steps in a biotech company if they believe in the medicine. You must possess a lot of patience, if you invest in biotech companies. Only if after all these years is positive news is coming out, your patience will be rewarded.

A good example is Galapagos, which incidentally is a favorite share of many private investors. Galapagos was a long time a considered company with a bright future. However, the years of waiting for results. Eventually Galapagos still came out with positive test results, causing the share price rose sharply. Investors who believed for years in the business, got their patience.

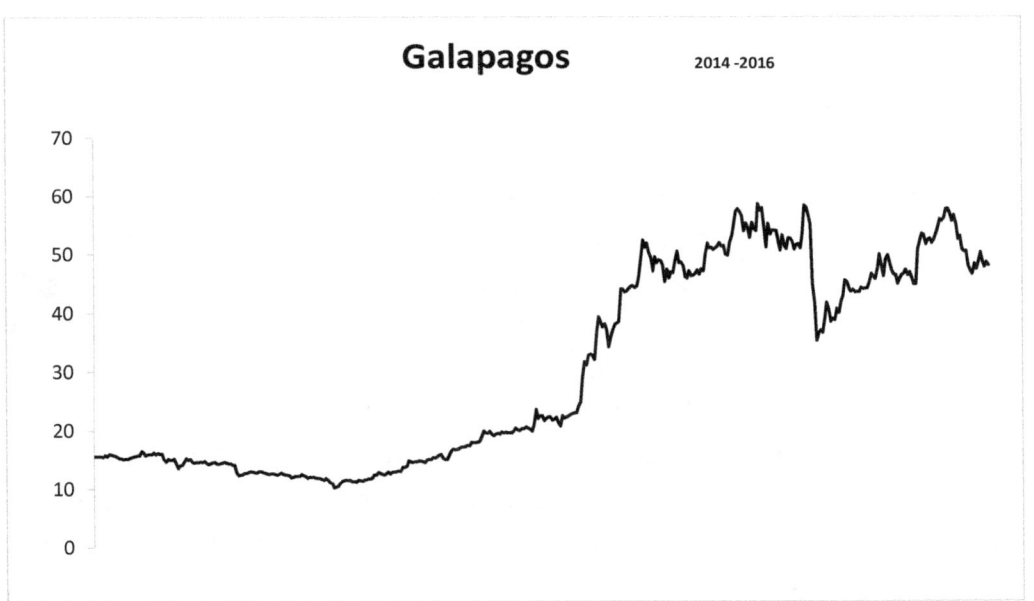

A company where the wait so far has yielded nothing, is Pharming. Although the company has put a product on the market, the price is low compare to the past. Mainly because of the many issues that did

Pharming, the current shareholders, the rate went down hard and there are still affected. The share is trading only a few cents.

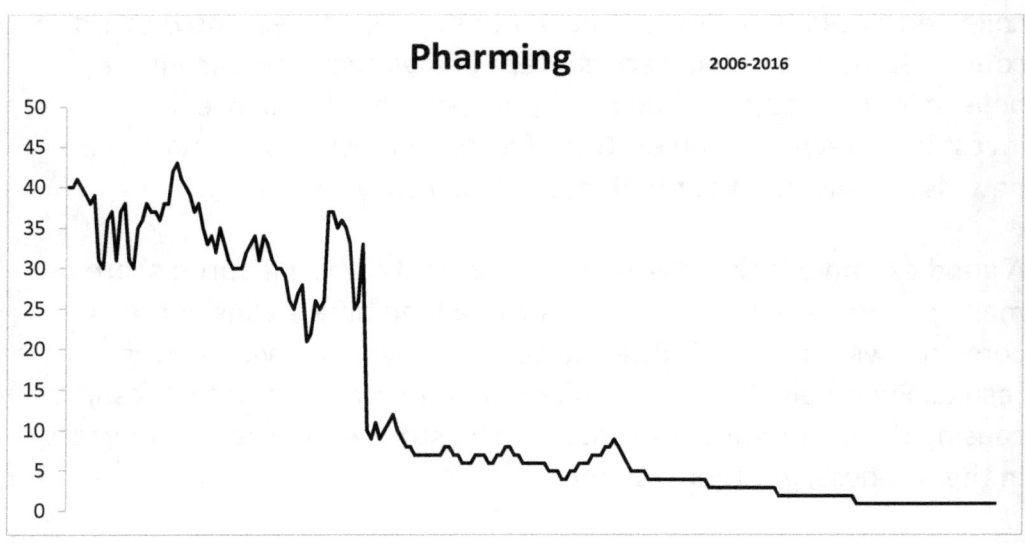

Right sales time

It is very difficult to determine when the perfect time to sell your shares. Only afterwards can you tell if you did well on your hold or sell shares. Prices change every day and it is almost impossible to sell the share at the highest price. It happens you maybe once or twice in your life, you sell at exactly the highest price level. Each investor gives himself a pat for it, but actually it's pure luck that you happened. All other times you do not sell at the highest point. And you have to accept things are like that. It is important to determine what has been selling decision. A great pillar, which you can use is by asking yourself the following question:

"Would I like to buy the stock at the current price?

If the answer is 'YES', then it is not a good time to sell the shares. Only if you need money immediately, that's an exception. If the answer is 'NO', then that is a reason to sell the stock. This rule is easy to apply on all your stock holdings. It prevents you from taking a decision on an emotional basis. If you're using this question it decides to sell, that's a decision that you take on a fundamental basis. You decide is whether you are valuing a stock is attractive or not attractive.

Technical analysis

A technical analysis is the study of historical prices combined with historical information from the market in order to make statements about future prices. With technical analysis you compare the current situation with a situation that has occurred in the past. And that analysis tells you how the stock is going to move now. Whether this comes out, it is always the question. Technical analysts are always right, because they always afterwards assess and explain the situation. Technical analysis is actually post your analysis right. With this statement, technical analysts will probably not totally agree, but it is, in my opinion, simply the reality.

In my first year at the stock exchange, I used a lot of technical analysis. Mainly because you are always right with technical analysis. Once I realized that the same always afterwards to explain, I am herewith partially stopped. My investment results based on technical analyzes were not always so rosy. Prices are simply impossible to predict, even in combination with historical data, as is done with technical analysis. Within this analysis, there are many indicators that determine the direction of the share price. However, I noticed that there are a number of price formations, technical analysis is actually profitable. The most reliable price patterns based on technical analysis, I discuss below.

Support and Resistance:
Support levels indicate the share price, which does the majority of investors, the shares from that point will go up. If the price falls

towards the support level and the share goes down, buyers will be more inclined to buy and sellers are less inclined to sell. Resistance levels indicate the share price, which does the majority of investors that prices will go down from that point. If the price rises towards the resistance levels, sellers will be more inclined to sell and buyers will be less likely to buy.

When a level of support is reached several times, the significance of the price level is thus stronger. The probability that the proportion falls through the border is getting smaller, because again and again shows that buyers and sellers decide that prices rise from there. With a resistance is exactly the same. A support level, it is therefore wise to buy a share and just sell near resistance. If a support or resistance is broken anyway, this is a strong sign to say goodbye to your position. When a support level is broken, it is wise to sell your shares, but if resistance is broken is to buy wisely right shares. There is a trend reversal.

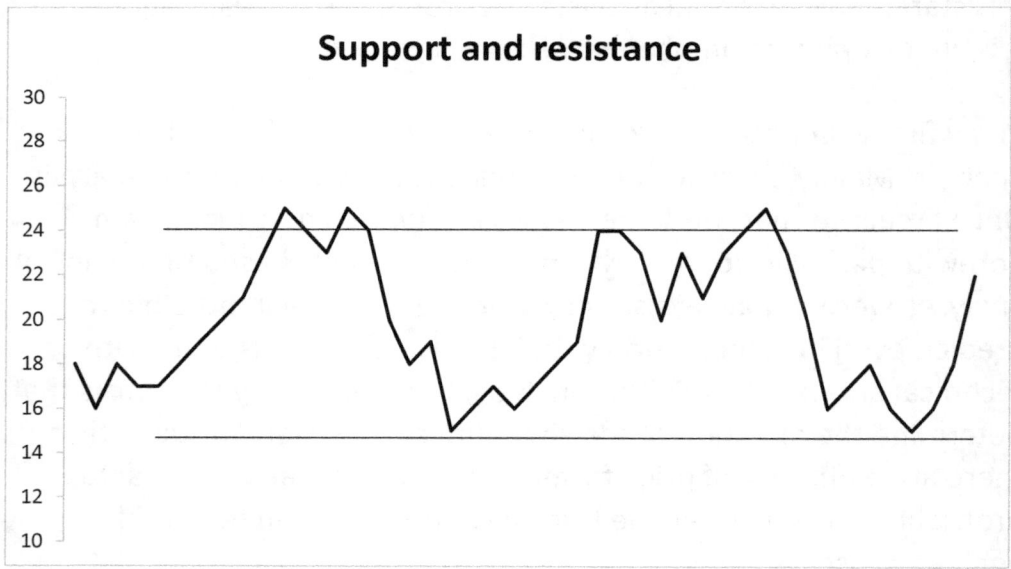

Double top and bottom:
A further step in the area of support and resistance levels are the double top and bottom. A double top is created when the share again returns after a drop to the previous peak and then decreases. There

are not enough buyers to raise the price above the previous high and sellers push the price down. A double top is a strong indication that an end to the upward trend. A double bottom is created when the share again returns after a rise to the previous low point and then rises again. The buyers have the upper hand and ensure that the price is falling trend does not continue. A double bottom is an indication that an end to the downward trend. Both a double bottom as a double top are reliable indicators, which often prove their service.

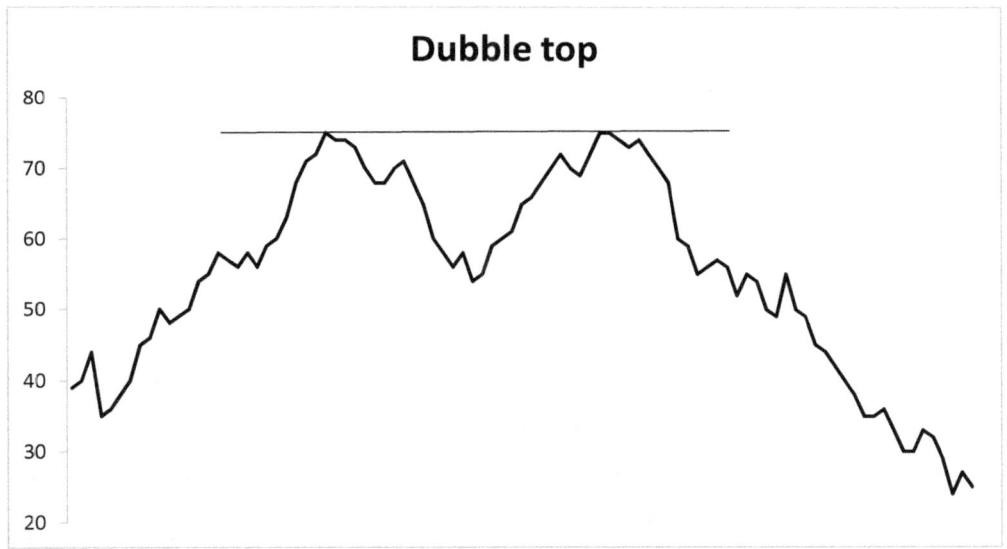

Trend line:
If the price is in an upward or downward trend, one often sees that there may be a second line drawn parallel to the trend line between the price moves back and forth. In a rising trend goes the second line along the tops of the share and in a downtrend which comes second line along the bottoms of the share. This is called trend lines. A trend line is a good tool to determine the purchase or sale point. May also trend lines except for the determination of the purchase and sale moments give significant signals. Such a signal is when price breaks out of the channel. Is that outbreak in the same direction as the trend, this is a trend for enhancing signal. The trend turns as it were in high gear. However, the price breaks through the other way

around, then this is a weakening trend. It is a first signal that the current trend is coming to an end.

"The trend is your friend"

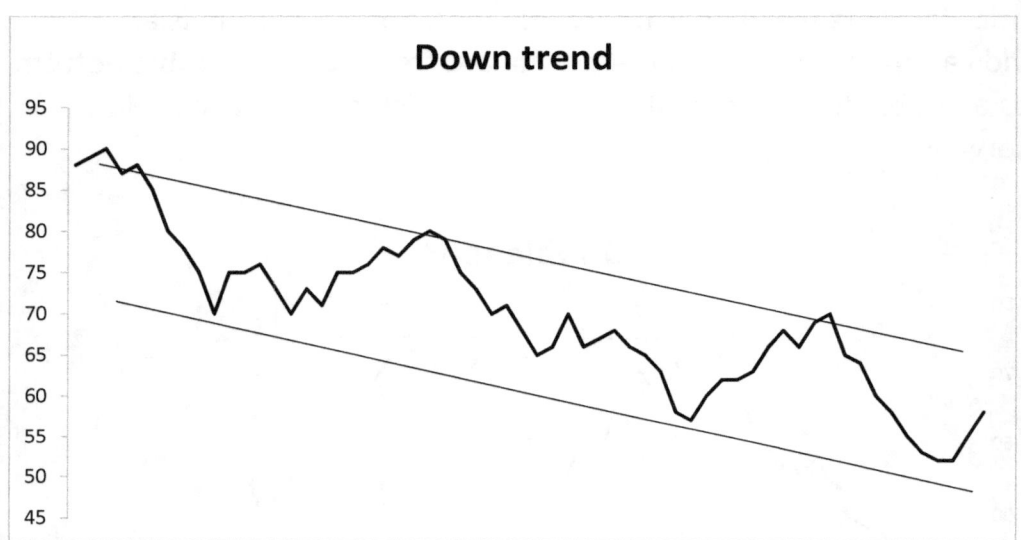

At this chart you can act as an investor. These are the most famous and reliable price patterns in technical analysis. The many other indicators in technical analysis I find much less reliable. Therefore you can use it more to a lesser extent.

Efficiency certificates

An investment, which is still relatively new, its calls efficiency certificates. With it you can still get profit on the maturity date at a higher price of the product in a sideways or downward market. This makes it a very interesting product. Efficiency certificates are just trading on the exchange. The product offers a fixed return if the price of the underlying value remains above a certain limit during the term, the efficiency frontier called. Note the share price at some point below the yield limit, the investor receives at maturity paid the closing price of the share. The only thing the investor thus has gone wrong, is receiving dividend. Efficiency certificates are available on equities and indices and have different maturities. The duration is usually around one year.

Example: You want to buy a return certificate on the share ASML. The share price is at time of writing € 83.93 (November 2015).
Buy 1 performance certificate ASML
Coverage Limit: € 68.50
Maximum payout: € 104.35
Deadline: February 19, 2016
Certificate course: € 98,50

You pay € 98.50 for the certificate. The share ASML, which at time of writing is € 83.93, the remaining 2.5 months may not at any time fall below the yield limit of € 68.50. That is 19% below the current price. Because the risk is relatively small, that that price development happens, the price of the certificate is near the payoff amount of € 104.35. When ASML does not fall below € 68.50, you will receive as the owner of the certificate € 104.35 return on February 19, 2016. Suppose the stock ASML does in the meantime fell over the border of tap € 68.50, you will receive the closing price of the share ASML on 19 February 2016. This is a price that does have a limit to the benefit limit of € 104,35. Only if the stock ASML above €68.50 remains scoring, the final payment is € 104.35.

6. Returning trade effects

Every year there are a number of recurring events at the stock exchange, which set the shares often in the same way move. Because these events are recurrent, investors can take advantage of these movements. Below I describe ten events that have a positive or a negative impact on equity. Of course there is never determine with certainty whether that events will happen in the future, as the same effect as in the past. It can be said that stands out, that by far the majority of cases the price effect does occur. The following examples can be used as signals to just buy stocks or even to sell in some cases.

Year-end effect

The year-end rally is a popular topic among investors each year. In September begin the first investors already talking about the phenomenon. The most frequently asked question is: "Will there again be a year-end rally this year?" The media hooks here only too happy and in newspapers and the Internet are from that time full of opinions and perspectives of investment professionals. Actually, everyone goes there automatically assume that a year-end rally will occur.

Especially the huge hype surrounding the year-end rally ensures that the rally gets going. Everyone wants to see once rising prices and everyone is prepared for it. The huge optimism of investors the markets often rise at the end of the year. The fact that analysts leave the light on in the coming year, creates positive feelings among investors. Analysts namely always positive about the coming year. Even if it is bad, they always see bright spots and buying opportunities. Analysts also ensure the positive effect at the end of the year.
The fact that everyone already assumes a year-end rally, ensures that investors continue to buy more shares to profit from the trend. In the

nineties a year-end rally was often used in the last two weeks of the year. The prices then increased by two weeks continuously. When everyone knew once that stock markets would rise the last two weeks, everyone wanted to be there early enough. Of course you want to buy as the first person to benefit from the entire increase. Because everyone wants to buy shares first, the start of the year-end rally is continually pushed forward. All those investors purchasing ensure that stock exchanges, at an earlier time than anyone had anticipated, rising. The disadvantage is that the end-of-year rally it also makes it ends earlier. The last two weeks of the year are now increasingly engaged to properly sell shares. It seems that today starts the year-end rally on the first trading day for December. From that day the last few years the stock exchanges walk firmly.

"In about 85% of the last decades, the AEX closing December with profits"

Professional market makers often close the books in December. They take positions smooth and often want no crooked equity positions anymore. This ensures that the last two weeks of December, the trade is very thin at the stock exchange. Professionals are no longer active in the acquisition of shares. They only want to trade from the new year on. And you can also benefit as a private investor about this.
On January 2 of each year, professional market participants want to step back on the stock exchange. After all, they have seized the last two weeks of December to take proper leave of their positions. After two weeks it's just time to rebuild equity positions. Therefore, the stock market usually rises on January 2 and the days, and even weeks, after. January is often a good month and determines the remainder of the year.

"How does January? So goes the year "

In recent years I backed myself with the January effect. On the last day of the year I buy shares or call options on the AEX. Which I sell then directly on January 2nd or subsequent days or weeks. It is, as always with investing, not always right, but by far the majority of cases I have achieved profits. The shares, which are often additional rise sharply on *January 2 effects*, are the small caps. These small stocks rise faster because the small size of these companies, but few buyers are required to produce a substantial capital gain. And there are often fewer vendors on January 2, so that the buyers by far in the majority. As a result, the exchange effect is enhanced. If you decide to buy options or long turbos, it is advisable not to take too many risks. With options, it is wise to choose a day options, but, for example the February series. With turbos is wise not to have to close the stop loss at the current rate. Although the chances are that prices rise, it is not wise to take unnecessarily high risks.

Company breakdown

Splitting a company often has a major positive impact on the share price. Under the motto: the parts are worth more than a whole, creates shareholder value. Often the hedge funds, which insist on the board of a company to split the company. Hedge Funds steps often in those shares as a reason to bring the undervaluation of the proportion of the light. For various reasons the share doesn't rise, causing the undervaluation of the company can persist for years.

"Individual parts are always worth more than if a company is integral"

When a company announces to split the company, it is often interesting to step in and buy shares directly. Often, the share rises the same day all over the news. The company may decide to split the entire company into equal pieces. The company may decide to dispose of an item and bring to the stock exchange. For example, Philips had in 2015 been able to bring the light division to the stock exchange. The value at which the division will go public, is in any case higher than the current value in Philips shares. It was therefore a good decision to buy directly the Philips share on the day of publication. Not entirely coincidentally, the stock rose that day. Then the wait, until the part is actually repelled. Around that day to take the wise profit by selling the share.

CEO buys shares

When the board of a company itself buys shares it is often a positive signal. The board finally knows the most about the ins and outs of the business. They know first how it goes and how the company's future looks like. Many details about the company are not taken out, so private investors take their decision to invest in the company does not agree with 100% information. The board has this information, and when they get in by buying shares, you can often sit back confidently. You've made the right decision to invest in that company.

Often increases the share price after the announcement that the CEO shares purchased. The CEO is boarded, often puts (temporarily) a floor under the price. This information can benefit you as a private investor to act thereon. It may be an additional confirmation to hold your shares instead of selling. Or you could buy the stock straight away.

Sometimes CEO`s buy shares when it goes bad with the company. They will try to convince the market that the future looks bright. That way CEO`s are trying to support the share price under pressure. In the summer of 2015, the CEO of Fagron purchased shares in order to notify the market that Fagron the lower price is a bargain. Nevertheless, half a year later, the proportion was still more than 70% lower than at the time of the purchase by the CEO. From this it is clear that this signal is not a 100% certainty provides to investors.

Company figures

The interim figures, companies presenting quarterly almost always provide a significant price movement. Therefore you can respond as an investor in different ways. Because you do not know in advance whether figures windfalls or even disappointing, it is not wise to bet on the direction of the stock. Gambling via a call option or put option so works just like in the casino. In some cases it is better to do both, a call and a put option to gamble: the so-called *long straddle*.

Investors are very interested in the development of a business because there previously was a lot of commotion around the company. As a result, the volatility of the share prior to the presentation of the figures probably been great. As a result, options become very expensive and often does not make sense to buy options. Usually the commotion is greater than was necessary. Therefore, the reaction of the share (positive or negative) on the figures often too moderate and much lower than previously thought.

Conversely, it also works. If previously little talk about the upcoming results of operations of a particular company, the volatility is not very big in advance. There is apparently nothing special expected and therefore the chance of a surprise is the greater. The result is that the share price after the announcement thereof, often moves significantly. The low expectations are option premiums (right to buy options) much more attractive. You can respond to this by buying a long straddle. This is a call option and a put option with the same strike price. If the stock then make a strong movement, it does not matter whether the price movement up or down. You benefit at least on one side then.

Just before the presentation of the interim results of Vopak in 2015 it was wise to buy a long straddle at a share price of around € 45,-. It is advisable to choose a series of short-term because you speculate for a short term. An option with a short term maturity less time / expectation money, and making it relatively more benefit from the intrinsic value, which builds the option that a violent price reaction after the business figures.

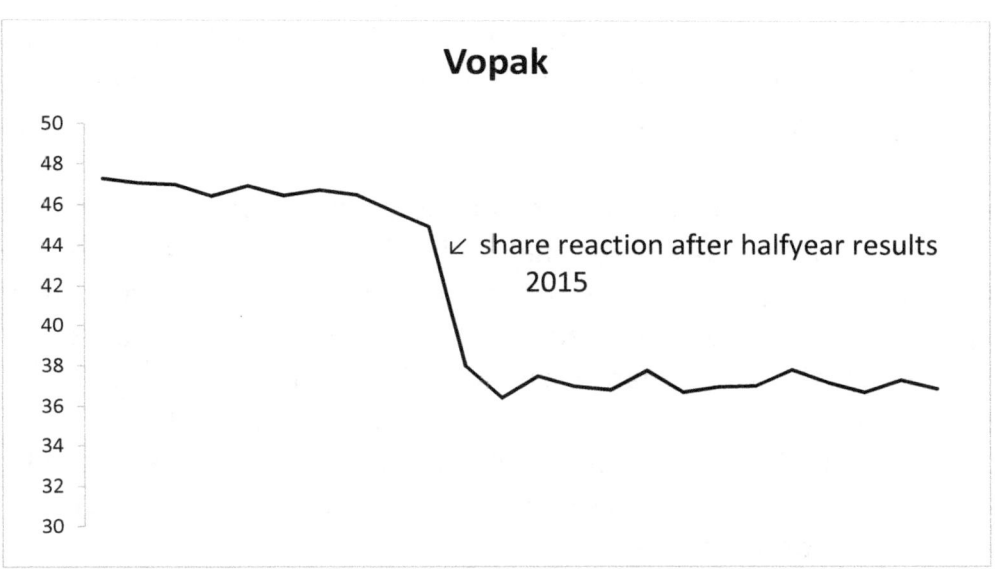

Buy call in September 2015, strike € 45, -, price € 1.20.
Buy well in September 2015, strike € 45, -, price € 1.30.

You bought this straddle for € 2.50, which can benefit both a falling and rising price. The option series had a remaining term of four weeks. Vopak's shares had to move sharply. With a share price above € 47.50 € 42.40 or under you make profit as an investor.

Vopak shares fell after the half-year figures to € 37, -.

Call option value: € 0.00.
Put option value: € 8.00.

This was the return € 5.50 (€ 8, - - € 2.50)

IPO

Subscribe to an IPO (Initial Public Offering) pays off in vast majority of cases. In some cases there is already on the first day the company goes public, made a hefty profit. It is for most companies a dream to go public. Companies listed on the stock exchange, are indeed big in sight. The *big boys* are all listed on the stock exchange. And every company wants to hear that.

There are several reasons why a company would go public. Often companies want to raise additional capital for a company to make a major growth spurt. The name recognition is an other great reason to go public. Ajax football club went public in 1998. It brought 28% of the shares to the Amsterdam Exchange. Ajax brought such a small percentage to the market, suggests that mainly concerned the reputation. The IPO has commercially nothing. Dividend the football club hardly pays out. This IPO is one of the few in which you as an investor had nothing to look for.

In recent years seem like entrepreneurs wanting to take their company public to want to *cash out*. The entrepreneurs have done their job to build a successful business from scratch and bring it at the height of the market to the stock market. This abbreviation is what the IPO may get a completely different meaning.

"It's Probably Overpriced"

The Samwer brothers are known as the most successful Internet entrepreneurs in Germany. They know from scratch to build a company and bring it to the stock market at the peak. Often, they do so copying of existing formulas. In the late nineties they copied to create the Ebay business by Alando. About three months later they sold the company to eBay for € 38 million. When it appeared that worked their copycat strategy, they decided to repeat it later in the year with different business models. The entrepreneurs copied to focus on the business formula of Zappos.com by Zalando. When it appeared that Zalando was a success, they brought Zalando with great fanfare for the top prize to the stock exchange. Zalando was one of the exceptions, the IPO was not successful. The share fell on the first day by 25%. Zalando was due to the enormous hype vastly *overpriced* .

Nevertheless, most IPO`s are worth investing in. Not all IPO`s are overpriced or not worth investing in. By far the majority of IPO`s can be booked a capital gain in the first week of trading. In other cases, the price remains the same. A huge loss-making IPO in the first week of trading, such as Zalando, rarely happens.

It therefore pays to participate in IPO`s. If you participate in ten different IPO`s and in the first week of trading of shares you sell, chances are huge that you have made profits. The price performance after the first week, will be hard to say. The effect of the IPO is then usually directly over and the craziness around as well. And it makes sense just to sell when everyone is still in the hype of the IPO.

Rumors

Stocks move as a result of an event. Actually, you can divide all events into two types: the facts and the rumors. Facts include operating results and press releases such as new orders and acquisitions. Facts are, compared to rumors, actually very rare. Rumors are, after all, every day. How often do you hear stories about potential acquisitions or problems at companies as a result of the slowdown in China or problems in Greece. The entire exchange trading is determined by rumors and conjecture, playing every day. That puts the stock price movement, just as investors buy or sell these rumors. And that they do by investors emotions *of fear* and *greed*. What is striking is that rumors stock prices affect much more than the actual facts.

"facts are stopping rumors"

In rumors investors are speculating about the impact, which has a potential event on the company. If then the actual figures are announced, the fun speculating is over. The share price then comes to rest again. Not for nothing is the exhibition saying property of the matter is the end of the entertainment.

With rumors are often exaggerated the price movement of the stock. Something that is seen as positive, leaving the share prices often rise much more robust than what is justified. And the same applies vice versa. This exaggerated reaction of the share can benefit investors by contrarian responding to the masses.

A good example is the smear, which, just before the third-quarter results that Pharming announced, originated in 2015. Investors were looking for sales of the product Rhucin. Because this is the only things what means that Pharming sells, the company has since fully dependent. In the weeks prior to the announcement of the third quarter figures, therefore, the voltage rose sharply. Previously there were rumors that the sale could be much better than expected. The share thus increased about 35% over that period. When the third quarter results were announced, the stock fell again. Sales of the drug Rhucin was excellent and was not totally bad. The fact that many investors had previously added accumulate the stock, caused the share had risen too far. Even with the strong sales of the drug Rhucin was the price increase of 35% greatly exaggerated. The share subsequently fell in the period by about 30%. Here was saying *possession of the matter is the end of the entertainment* certainly applicable.

The figures were known and fantasy disappeared from the stock. Because in the period thereafter probably nothing to do with the stock, investors sell back their shares, making stock prices back down after disclosure of the facts. It is therefore wise to rumors which make the share price rise, you just sell shares. Take that price gains with it, because if there is actually good news, what the market will surprise comes, is uncertain. The market may be surprised, but in most cases this is not so. By *Taking profits no one has become poorer* is another appropriate adage.

Issue new shares

When a company announces to want to do a issue, you'd better sell your shares directly. In the short term the share nearly always declines very hard. The chance is very small that the price at which the publication of issuing was announced is still comes back, is the question. It usually takes a lot of time if that will happen.

"Issuing shares? Sell direct your shares !! "

Both rumors about an issue, as the actual publication of emissions, provide a firm falling share price. The company raises funds by issuing shares to the detriment of the existing shareholders. They should indeed include dividing shareholders profit after the emission. It is so much less attractive to possess the share and the price drops by it is quite logical.

Sometimes gives the company shares to accelerate the growth of the company. The company needs money for certain studies, building the product or taking over another company. This is a positive basis for making an emission. The issue is in fact done in order to make more satisfied current shareholders in the future to make more profit. However, there is another issue form, which is seen as negative. If a company's emissions *need* to do to solve problems, it has a much more negative effect on the share price. This form is because no raised money to grow, but to stay alive. Here, the current shareholder has actually nothing, except that he consequently lost all his money is not now.

Good examples from 2015, a company's emissions *need* to do to stay alive, are Ballast Nedam and Imtech. Both companies report ensured that stock prices ended up in a free fall. Both had to issue a lot of shares. The chance that this type of company stock price once again as high as on the emission date is virtually eliminated. Even when announcing the share issue collapsing immediately, it is wise to say goodbye to your equity. The probability that the price then drops even more, is enormous.

Rumors of an emission can really put pressure on a stock. With the publication of the quarterly figures of Delta Lloyd turned out to be solvency pressure. That surprised the market significantly. As Delta Lloyd by Solvency II was to improve solvency, there were rumors that Delta Lloyd had to come up with an emission. The share dropped from
€ 16, - within a short period to € 12, -. Because at a lower price, more shares had to be issued, would be the consequences of an emission at a price of € 12, - are greater than € 16, -. This negative momentum made Delta Lloyd slid to € 6, -. This price Delta Lloyd announced to do an issue. Because at a price of € 6, - dilution is even greater, the existing shareholders have a huge loss. The question is when the old price of € 16, -, when the rumor was known about an issue, is again reached. It can do long time in coming.

Therefore, it is almost always very wise to sell your shares directly, when messages appear about a possible issue. Only after the issue it is often wise again to pick up the shares. Often then reached the lowest share price and characterize investors and analysts the stock as a bargain.

High volume

When in a company significantly more shares traded than is normally the case, the increase or decrease is more meaningful. This is because there is more enthusiasm for the chosen movement. This is because more investors are devoted to the same opinion. Chances are that the rest of the audience follows the direction of the stock. Certainly with a large price movement has a large volume much effect. After a first day of trading with sharp price movements and thereby a large trading volume, we usually see in the days that

followed the same pattern. To weeks or even months after the first day can continue this movement.
The reason for a large volatility, together with a higher than average volume, are typically company figures, acquisition rumors and failures.

"A large price movement is more effective with large volume"

A good example is the proportion of AND International Publishers, listed on the Amsterdam stock exchange.
Friday, November 27, 2015 the share price closed at € 6.27. The days before the race is remarkably increasing, with gains of between 2% and 8% per day. The volume in the share is not to mention remarkably high. The volume was 28,022 shares, which is slightly higher than normal. Nothing strange, but investors on investment forums have began to wonder if something was playing on.

The days that followed were as follows:

Monday, November 30: closing rate € 6.75 (7.6% capital gain)
Turnover: 43 545 shares
Tuesday, December 1: closing price € 7.73 (14.5% capital gain)
Turnover: 86 522 shares
Wednesday, December 2: closing price € 8.94 (15.6% capital gain)
Turnover: 261 358 shares

Investors were on Friday, November 27th all be right, because there actually played something by AND. On Monday, namely increased share accompanied by an increasing volume again. This volume was higher than average. More and more buyers participated in this increase, the week before it was deployed. The movement, which made the stock AND northward, was reinforced by the large volume in the stock. The fact that more and more buyers join the increase indicates that the movement has a lot of meaning. It played anything

but showed reactions to investment forums that no one knew what was going on.
Tuesday, December 1, the share was again on a large volume up. The sequel to the rise Monday was not strange. There were a lot of the buyers active.

On Wednesday, December 2nd it was announced that AND takeover talks conducted with several parties. That was the reason why the price and volume rose so much. When shares without news, with increasing large volume, there are still investors who often know more about it. These are the investors, who are close to the fire. Or are insiders in the company, news have leaked to certain people or parties. This kind of practice is rare to light, despite many studies by AFM. It happens almost daily, that suspiciously shares traded in a particular stock, which then rises or falls sharply. Only days after news comes out about what is actually going on. Many private investors then run behind the facts, while the price movement has been largely completed.
It is therefore wise to keep an eye on the trading volume of shares. The larger the volume, the more meaning the appreciation or depreciation. And without news is brought out, can you as individual investor anticipate.

Short parties

Beware of shares in which many hedge funds are short. *Short* means that you sold shares, you do not have in your possession. Hedge Funds, which are short, therefore suggests that the stock price will drop, and then buy back at a lower price those shares.

Hedge Funds are not just short in a share for no reason. They only decide to go short, as they have a strong suspicion that something is not quite right with the company. Professionals have information and resources which do not have private investors. Therefore it is wise to seriously consider whether you want to buy a share or possess if it appears that many hedge funds are short. Chances are strong that the company concerned to publish negative news, which is not good in any case for the share.

Often, it is the hedge funds itself, which take care of further price pressure. They sell a lot of shares, resulting in a decline in the share price. Hedge Funds have computer programs that surreptitiously sell shares, with a declining rate as a result. This sentiment is negative about the company concerned and the media throw a little extra with their suspicion that something negative will play in the company. Rumors of bad news ensure that the vicious circle of the share price, which has long remains under selling pressure around. You often see this in any claim emissions. If an impending issue, go hedge funds shorting the stock and increase the proportion of their marketing programs even further, making the final issue price is even lower. This creates further dilution, hedge funds buy back shares again at the issue price and have taken a big profit.

Delta Lloyd is beautifully portrayed. Two chapters returned you have read that example.

At time of writing (late 2015), the top ten short positions in Dutch shares are as follows:

- *9.99 % SBM Offshore: Expect high penalty in Brazil*
- *9.72 % Air France-KLM: huge competitive sector*

- 5.70 % Fugro: enormous problems oil industry
- 5.38 % Aperam : poor commodity market
- 5.01 % Arcelor Mittal : poor commodity market
- 4.22 % PostNL: slumping postal
- 2.99 % Delta Lloyd: expect big issue solvency
- 2.15 % Heijmans: financial problems
- 1.92 % Imtech: bankruptcy
- 1.29 % Galapagos : overstatement

In all of these companies plays negative news and hedge funds think so that developments are worse than the market expected.

Round numbers

History shows that round numbers inspire people to make decisions. It is a special phenomenon that share prices always move to round numbers. The law of round numbers has to do with pure emotion. Investors would like namely, that the round number comes at the price board. And if all the buyers and sellers are willing, then moves the price there by investors naturally to. The law of round numbers is one of the most reliable events at the stock exchange. I wonder here, since I began investing, over.

Why investors are so eager to see a round number on the board rate is not straightforward to explain. Investors probably see the round number as the next price target, both upwards and downwards. A target price, which is always bound to be met. If the relevant price target is reached, the share or index often remains floating around for a while that number. Investors are struggling with it, before a decision is taken to break the round number to north or south.

"The reliability around price levels, is especially interesting when the price level never or for a long time has not been reached"

If the share rises towards the round number, investors want to take profits on the round number. Many investors see it as a target and thus the maximum of a share. And everyone wants the summit to sell his shares, hence the order book is full of sell orders at the round price level. This works the other way exactly that same. If a stock goes down towards the round number many purchase orders will be at minimum. After all, investors believe that the round number is the target and thereby also the base price for the share. And every investor wants to buy the stock at the bottom of the market, so the order book is full of buy orders.

There are many examples to think of stocks and indices, struggling with a round figure. A good example was the AEX index, which rose to 500 points. That happened in March 2015.

Leading up to the 500 points mark was there in all the media attention to the moment when this limit would be reached. The AEX was in an upward trend since January 2015. The closer the 500 points, the slower the upward trend. Investors know that this score is the price target of many investors, and therefore many investors on the state of 500 points to sell their investments. Investors who do not want to wait until exactly 500 points, sell slightly earlier their shares, just below the level of 500 points. This ensures that the upward trend decreases as the race gets closer around a price level.

"It's not a question 'if' but 'when' the round price level is reached"

When the AEX in March 2015 reached the 500 points mark, it fell directly down 500. The first contact with the 500 point threshold drew a lot of vendors to sell all their shares. After a week to have the 500 points nosed, AEX decided to come here for respite to sag slightly. From there, the index pulled new buyers again to find enough strength to break through the 500 point threshold. This force is synonymous motion investors. It took about a month to break the 500 points limit. Basically the 500 score nothing special, but the emotion of investors took this round figure to many difficulties.

The law of round numbers will always be there and private investors may anticipate. If a stock or index close to a state round number, you know almost certain that there will be a motion to this price level. When the AEX stood at 425 points, no one was concerned with the question of when the AEX would be at 500 points. But in an uptrend, where the AEX is at 490 points and the round price level never or a long time has not been touched, you know that all investors have that number in their head. And if that is the case, the question is not *whether* but *when* the round number is reached. On a stand of 490 points I am therefore at that time long gone by buying call options with a long duration. That is something investors can do in the future, when the AEX example, for the first time is close to 600 or 700 points is.

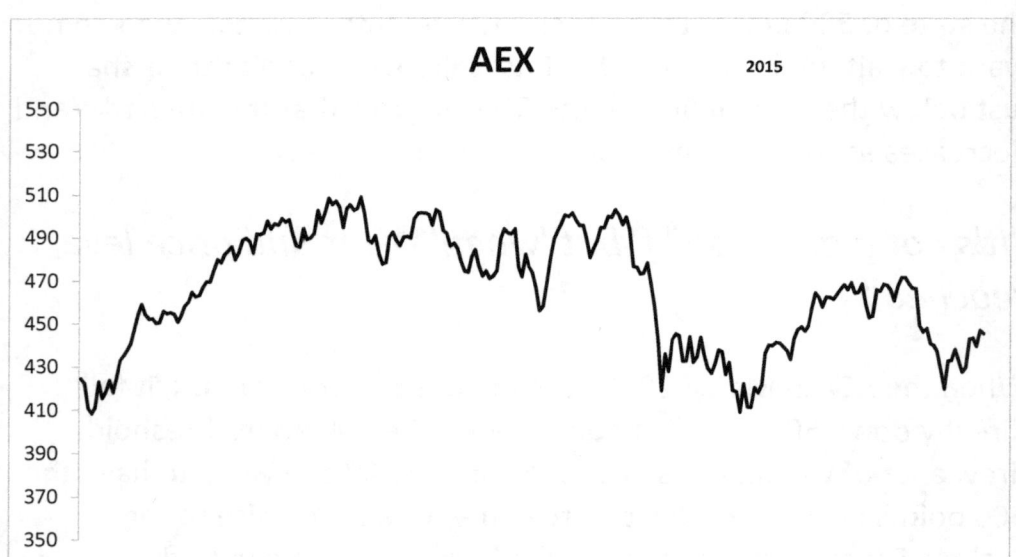

7. My investments

I have in the first chapter provides a summary of the most common mistakes investors take. Unfortunately, the majority of the investors making these errors. Sometimes investors see quickly that this is not the right way of investing. In other cases, it sometimes takes years before an investor has known by this. So it was with me that same. It is never too late to change strategy and to swap the gambling in investments based on profit. So I had a lot of good and bad experiences over the years. In total I have done over 2000 transactions since I started on my twelfth investing.

I started investing in the nineties. In hindsight the nineties was not a good time to invest learning investing. At that time stocks rose in a straight upward trend channel. And that trend has been maintained for years. The striking fact was that rose all the shares and it did not matter what business you put your money. The shares eventually rose anyway. However, one share increased slightly harder than the other. You knew if investors no fear of losing, because it was almost impossible. My first investment was the purchase of a mutual fund. I got on my twelfth a letter from Postbank, which had launched a new mutual fund. As a regular customer of Postbank should I invest free of charge and that I have done. It was the introduction of Postbank IT fund. That was the first mutual fund in the hype, which was to follow. So a few months later there followed the Postbank Internet Fund, Media Fund and a number of other computer based funds in the hype. The number of mutual funds of Postbank was extended from five pieces to two dozen in a short time. That was in hindsight a clear signal that there was a hype. But at the very moment one had still by and seemed to grow trees to the sky. I bought the Postbank IT Fund at a price of ƒ 50, -. A few weeks later I sold the fund's at a price of ƒ 56, -. I made 12% return within weeks. My first investment income was a fact. I became an investor, or so I thought. Actually this was the beginning of my hobby as a speculator, other name of gambler. That is quite different from investing, it became clear to me afterwards.

After about a year to have acted in mutual funds, I decided to take the plunge into single shares. My uncle had explained at that time that I at least need ƒ 1000 - to go to the stock market. Only then was, by then still high commission costs, investments profitable. I thought as a thirteen year old boy first, that there is a minimum limit was set by the market, but in retrospect I understood that my uncle mentioned the cost efficient. I had little feeling at the time to determine what share I could buy the best. In 1997 it all stocks rose anyway, so choose either only one out. Eventually I left my decision depend on the analyst recommendations, which I found on teletext. The price targets for the stock ASML and Baan Company were highest. The price targets for the share of Baan Company were supreme, so I decided to choose this share. I bought the share at a price of ƒ 88, -. Not much later after my purchase it went wrong. In the quarterly figures, which announced the company revealed that the first was not as good as imagined in years. The figures were disappointing and the stock fell hard. A week later I sold the stock. A painful loss, but in retrospect was one of my best ever investment decisions. The shares would then have collapsed much further. It no longer came to the company Baan Company and was acquired in 2000 by the British Invensys. In retrospect, also particularly in order to establish how different the process can work. In the year 1995 the shares ASML and Baan Company equally popular among private investors. Baan Company has not survived the hype, while ASML just then as best performed at the stock exchange. ASML is to this day still the best performing stock on the Amsterdam stock exchange today.

My worst investment ever was an investment in the stock AND. In 2010 I bought the share at € 4.45, which afterwards in that period the height turned out to be. I made my decision again depend on analysts opinions. The share would be undervalued and share doubling lay ahead. Instead of doubling the rate was half a year later, there is a half price. Fearing a further decline in the price I decided to

sell my shares at a price of
€ 2.22. The share slumped the following months further to below € 1,
-. As an investor softens yet the pain you have suffered the loss,
because it could have ended worse. Anyway, I learned an important
lesson after this investment. I finally stopped with the value I
attached to analysts opinions. My experience taught me that I often
advised the opposite of what analysts should do.

When I now look to the AND share, there is a price of more than
€10,- on the board. Investing long term often pays better than acting
prematurely. A good example of this is again.

My best investment ever by speculating on short-term call options in
DSM. I bought in 2005, short-term call options, because I based on
technical analysis expected the DSM share would increase. I saw a
bottom pattern, but eventually it took a long time before something
happened. For weeks I held my position. At one point there was
going only a week. My call options would expire within five days, so I
had time to decide what I would do. I was on that day behind my
computer at home to watch the share price. It was pretty boring,
because there was no movement. The share was between € 50,50
and € 51, -. At that time it was dealt with nickels, and pennies or not
tenths of cents, as is currently the case. Suddenly, the share rose
sharply to € 51.10. I thought, that was a big buyer. After that the
share of less than five seconds later to € 51.40, including large
volume. I knew immediately that something was going on, because
such rapid movement up among large volume indicates something.
Less than ten minutes later the share was € 54,10. My heart was
racing, and my call options were suddenly worth a fortune. All day,
the value of my options below my purchase price of € 1.000, - but
suddenly they were € 4.500, - worth. A profit of € 3.500, - or 350% in
a couple of minutes! The proportion was huge so I took my phone
and so I decided to sell my position immediately. An hour later came
DSM with a press release that it increases the profit forecast for the
remainder of the year. That report the stock rose the next day

towards € 56, -. At that price, I had € 3,000- additional profit may have, but I was certainly happy with the € 3.500, -.

The DSM share was also one of my favorite stocks. Everyone has a stock, where he or she has with most feeling with. A share where you like to invest in. Often this is because you have achieved good investment results, and understands the price trend. It is therefore to be careful not to fall in love with a stock, because that can make you hold the stock, even in times when bad times coming up with the company. It is better to look at what your investment at that particular moment have the best chance of winning. From gut feeling investors often opt for a stock, where they have invested in previously. They seem to have a relation to this. I had actually not much with the company DSM, but I found the movement of the share very nice. Other shares I liked very much, were Hagemeyer, KNP BT, World Online and Libertel. The latter was my absolute favorite stock. The volatility of these stocks were very large and therefore interesting to follow. Namely that offered great opportunities for *trading* . Even with World Online I made a modest profit. World Online was exactly at the height of the dotcom bubble going the stock market. The share declined since its IPO of € 43,- to € 12,-. I bought the shares for € 15,25, then two weeks later sold it for € 16,20.

Today, I have no favorite share anymore. That's because I try as much as possible to act according to my strategy, so do not hold shares. Multiple polls and appears on investment forums, many retail investors do have favorite stocks. Thus, the shares Galapagos and TomTom often are loved. This is evident from the many followers on forums and in polls on websites. For both companies, there are great opportunities for the future. Galapagos can break with the launch of a rheumatoid arthritis drug and TomTom is considered an important part in the self-propelled vehicle.

Because I traded much, it often happened that I missed out profit, because I sold my investment too early. In 2007 I had the Stork shares call options with short maturities. I had a minimal profit and decided to take profits and thus sell my call options. Because I felt that, until the expiry date of my call options, there would be little movement in the share. In order not to lose I would better sell my position. However, something happened that I had no control over. A day after, the British-based investor Candover made an offer of € 47, - for Stork. I sold the day before my position for € 2.000, -. Had I waited another day, my position was approximately € 16,000, - been worth it. I hit me on my head, but who could have known that exactly that day a bid came in. It was bad luck, pure bad luck. And therefore very costly breakdown. The disadvantage of frequently changing stocks is that you can overcome such situations.

Nevertheless, there is another investment, where I could make more money with. During the credit crisis what started in 2008, I bought the US bank shares Fifth Third Bank Corporation in January 2009. The share was at a high of $ 42 in 2007 - but the credit crisis brought the share to a lowest point: $ 1.01. I bought the stock at $ 1.11 and sold it a week later for $ 1.50. An excellent return of almost 40%, which I was obviously very happy with. I appeared to have bought at the bottom, because the proportion ran weekly $ 1 - in. Within four weeks, the share was even at $ 6 – and a year later the shares were trading at $ 15 already. In 2014 the share had a high of $ 24, - !! If I had held the shares for a year, so I had to have a yield of 1250%. I had my entire investment budget of $ 6.000 - used and so a year later, an amount of $ 81.000, - I could have. Because it was an irresponsible position, because I had put my entire balance in one share, I sold too early from the position of fear. With the wisdom of now I would for a much smaller amount purchased shares, which would have taken much longer without fear of the share. Again it was a good learning experience for me. So I would have taken much longer without fear to keep the share.

Acquisitions and mergers are many times happening. You see on the next page, a newspaper from 1995. How many shares you remember from this period? In the meantime, there are many companies went bankrupt, acquired, merged or downgraded to a lower index.

BEURS VAN A

HOOFDFONDSEN

Dividend	Naam	GIM	V.krs.	L.krs.	H.krs.
94 3,20	ABN Amro	A++	58,60	58,60	59,20
94 4,85	Aegon	A++	123,70	124,00	125,90
94 0,77	Ahold	A	53,90d	53,50	54,60
94 7,00	Akzo Nobel	A++	188,00	189,30	191,40
94 1,28	Bols Wes.	A++	33,80	33,30	33,80
93/94 1,50	CSM c.	A++	67,40	67,20	68,10
94 8,76	Dordt. Petr.	-	211,00	212,80	214,30
94 6,00	DSM	A+	132,10	131,50	133,50
94 0,546	Elsevier	A++	18,10	18,10	18,30
91 0,75	Fokker	C	11,60	11,20	11,60
94 3,80	Fortis AMEV	A++	85,70	85,70	89,00
94 1,50	Gist-Broc.	A++	39,30	38,80	39,70
94 3,50	Heineken	A++	224,50	224,20	226,10
94 2,00	Hoogovens	A	63,20	63,10	64,20
94 2,00	H.Douglas	A	73,00	71,60	73,20
94 3,75	ING	A++	85,70	85,70	86,40
91/92 1,00	KLM	B+	49,60	49,50	50,00
94 1,00	KNP BT	B++	49,70	49,70	50,40
94 8,85	Kon. Olie	A++	197,00	198,50	200,30
94/95 2,30	KPN	A++	56,00	55,50	57,00
89 3,30	Nedlloyd	B+	57,00	54,30	58,4
94 2,25	Océ Grinten	B++	83,00	82,70	84,1
94 1,60	Pakhoed	A+	47,40	47,10	47,8
94 1,25	Philips	A	63,30	63,40	64,3
94 0,85	Polygram	A++	88,10	88,00	89,2
94 1,10	Stork	A	43,90	43,80	44,
94 4,71	Unilever	A++	196,70	197,60	198,
94 1,50	v.Ommeren	B++	47,50	47,40	47
94 4,00	VNU	A++	181,60	182,10	184
94 1,80	Wolters-K.	A++	127,30	127,50	129

Looking back on how I invested in the past, I see that it had nothing to do with investing. It was pure and only speculating, that is the same as gambling in a casino. I have made faults, as described in the first chapter of this book. It would have been much better to monthly small part to invest in the long term. I emphasize *a small part* , because it ensures that the interest is less for you, so you can keep investor emotions much better control. And that is investing for the long term is a prerequisite. Unnoticed build a robust power with a small monthly investment after years.

I have learned from my mistakes and invest now a lot quieter. I strive not to tower high returns and be content faster. I use a stop-loss on my investment that I lose cutoff. Furthermore, my capital invested proportionately much smaller than before. I think it is important to maintain a minimum 50% savings, regardless of the level of interest. The interest rate I do not see as important, because security must be in savings in the first place. By your savings account after holding the hand much of your ability, you become less dependent on your investments, so I find that I can better keep my investors motion under control. Accepting loss and unfreeze gains easier. Both profit and loss should not affect your trading behavior and I have pretty much under control.

My own investment plan is fully dedicated to control and clarity. I focus my while not on income, but mainly on following the investment plan. My main rules:

- Not more than 10% of the value of the investment portfolio per share (with a minimum of € 1.000,-).

- More than 50 % of the assets invested in shares of solid companies.

- Invested assets never exceeds the power of the savings account.

- Monthly writing short term call option on solid stocks.

- With each new equity investment directly a stop loss use an average of 10% .

- With about 15% of the investment portfolio trading in options and turbo ' s (see also the section entitled "recurrent rate effects").

- With persistent rumors of an emission sell the share.

- When newspapers are filled with large, negative headlines buy solid equity at lowered prices.

- At times, that newspapers tremendously positive about equities messages, just sell at higher prices.

- In the meantime, do not act and just quietly sitting back and not stare at stock prices .

Based on my investment plan I take relatively little risk. But I ensure adequate diversification and investment fun. My investment plan is mostly dominated by risk control and lean. The time needs to do its job. And that makes me between doing no unnecessary trades. The time will also ensure that you allow to raise the share, to receive dividends, option premium and even to profit in some cases a bid on your stock from an other company.

8. Epilogue

You've read in this book, that investor's emotions have much influence on the final investment result. Private investors often do the opposite of how you as an investor should trade correctly. Especially the media have an important influence. Knowledge about investing, you can gain in several ways. However, investors to keep emotions under control is a whole lot harder. The biggest enemy of investment, is therefor yourself. You are the one who is making wrong decisions by emotions. And that's just wrong. Everybody makes a mistake, so you have a loss. Everyone leaves sometimes trade opportunities. That once heard now on. Try the tips in this book to keep emotions under control.

Create an investment plan, which will show that you do not make the same mistakes, as 80% of private investors does. In the first chapter you read what mistakes that are.

With this book I hope to have made enough building blocks to create or adjust your personal investment plan. I am convinced that you can make a successful investment plan with the information in this book. Do this based on your investment horizon and risk you want to take.

Then choose how you want to divide your portfolio across regions, sectors, stocks and derivative investment products. Then you can select the companies you want to invest. Then make clear agreements with yourself: what criteria do you like at when deciding whether you are buying an investment, holding or selling. This can be done using the tips in this book.

Guarantees on profits do not exist, not even a good investment plan. No one can advance to determine with certainty which way stock prices move up. But I am convinced that the chance is much greater for the long-term returns with a solid investment plan is when you have no investment plan and trade in the issues of the day recklessly speculates. You can always refine your investment plan, but give your investment plan a chance to prove itself. If you still are not satisfied, you can adjust your plan bit by bit. Your investment plan ensures that you keep your emotions under control. And that's what I want to emphasize with this book.

Thank you for reading this book and I wish you good luck, joy and wisdom in investing.

www.ingramcontent.com/pod-product-compliance
Lightning Source LLC
Chambersburg PA
CBHW070306230526
45470CB00002B/747